History of Egypt

A Captivating Guide to Egyptian History, Starting from Ancient Egypt and the Nile through the Persians, Alexander the Great, and the Ottoman Empire to the Present

© Copyright 2025 - All rights reserved.

The content contained within this book may not be reproduced, duplicated, or transmitted without direct written permission from the author or the publisher.

Under no circumstances will any blame or legal responsibility be held against the publisher, or author, for any damages, reparation, or monetary loss due to the information contained within this book, either directly or indirectly.

Legal Notice:

This book is copyright protected. It is only for personal use. You cannot amend, distribute, sell, use, quote, or paraphrase any part, or the content within this book, without the consent of the author or publisher.

Disclaimer Notice:

Please note the information contained within this document is for educational and entertainment purposes only. All effort has been executed to present accurate, up-to-date, reliable, and complete information. No warranties of any kind are declared or implied. Readers acknowledge that the author is not engaging in the rendering of legal, financial, medical, or professional advice. The content within this book has been derived from various sources. Please consult a licensed professional before attempting any techniques outlined in this book.

By reading this document, the reader agrees that under no circumstances is the author responsible for any losses, direct or indirect, that are incurred as a result of the use of the information contained within this document, including, but not limited to, errors, omissions, or inaccuracies.

Free Bonus from Captivating History (Available for a Limited time)

Hi History Lovers!

Now you have a chance to join our exclusive history list so you can get your first history ebook for free as well as discounts and a potential to get more history books for free!

Simply visit the link below to join.

Or, Scan the QR code!

captivatinghistory.com/ebook

Also, make sure to follow us on Facebook, X, and YouTube by searching for Captivating History.

Table of Contents

INTRODUCTION 1
CHAPTER ONE – THE ORIGINS OF EGYPT..................................... 4
CHAPTER TWO – THE OLD KINGDOM.. 13
CHAPTER THREE – THE MIDDLE KINGDOM 26
CHAPTER FOUR – THE NEW KQINGDOM...................................... 41
CHAPTER FIVE – PERSIAN, GREEK, AND ROMAN EGYPT 76
CHAPTER SIX – MEDIEVAL EGYPT.. 101
CHAPTER SEVEN – THE OTTOMANS AND EARLY MODERN
EGYPT 119
CHAPTER EIGHT – MODERN EGYPT 144
CONCLUSION – THE ARAB SPRING AND THE FUTURE OF EGYPT 161
HERE'S ANOTHER BOOK BY CAPTIVATING HISTORY THAT YOU
MIGHT LIKE 164
FREE BONUS FROM CAPTIVATING HISTORY (AVAILABLE FOR A
LIMITED TIME) 165
SOURCES 166
IMAGE SOURCES 168

Introduction

With a population of about one hundred million people from different social and cultural backgrounds, a rich landscape, and a bustling life and culture, Egypt is one of the most interesting places on earth today. For the average visitor, Egypt may bring to mind its beautiful beaches, unique social structure, or history with pyramids and pharaohs. In contrast to modern Egypt's many attractions, there persists the image of an old civilization that dominated the region and produced some of the most remarkable cultural and material legacies to this day.

There is a good reason for that—only a few civilizations can claim to have had as great of an impact on human history as Egypt. The Nile River Valley, with its many gifts and curses, gave rise to a political powerhouse thousands of years ago that stood firm despite many domestic and outside challenges. It also gave rise to one of the most memorable and earliest societies at a time when humans were just beginning their transition from primitive to more complex ways of life. Aside from military and political power, this complexity was also manifested in a set of distinct traditions, customs, and, above all, people who have managed to retain their uniqueness after so many millennia.

The history of Egypt, thus, is complicated and extensive. Maybe its complicated nature stems from the fact that what we can call the first Egyptian state or society emerged long ago. Ancient Egypt has, without a doubt, one of the most captivating stories in world history. The astonishing ancient Egyptian myths and the memorable pantheon of deities shaped ancient Egyptian life and played a role in the formation and development of Western civilizations. Neighboring Mediterranean cultures, still relatively primitive in many respects and certainly weaker in political terms, were exposed to the might of Egypt through different means, thanks to Egypt's "head start" when it came to the process of civilization and development.

The role of ancient Egypt should not be understated, as there are many good reasons why it still is one of the most widely known periods of Egyptian history today. However, there is much more to the history of Egypt than the ancient era. After thousands of years of cultural and political domination and advancement, Egyptian history took an interesting turn. For hundreds of years, it grew closer to other civilizations that had begun to catch up and, in most cases, challenged Egypt. Egypt became a battlefield of many different empires, which were led by ambitious conquerors who wanted to gain hold of Egypt's valuable lands for themselves. Egypt was confronted with adversaries from Greece, Rome, the Levant, Persia, Arabia, and Anatolia. As they came and left, they left a lasting impact on Egypt, as they hoped to integrate it into their vast empires. In turn, this led to Egypt losing its flair and most of its material and immaterial heritage, something that was only relatively recently rediscovered when concentrated efforts were directed at exploring it.

By the late ancient era, Egypt had become part of the largest cosmopolitan sphere that had emerged in Europe—the Roman Empire. Egypt rapidly became one of the most integral parts of the empire. This also meant that Egypt was one of the earliest centers of Christianity, playing a pivotal role in the development of the religion that is at the basis of modern Western civilizations. It was through these interactions that Egypt transitioned into medieval times, during which it began to be dominated by the most powerful cultural force that has ever emerged from the Near East: Islam. Egypt was one of the first major regions to be Islamized by Arabs, who brought with them a distinct identity that has remained an inseparable part of Egyptian life ever since. After centuries, the religion managed to seamlessly merge with the local cultural heritage and way of life.

Throughout the Middle Ages, Egypt had to navigate its way through one of the most turbulent and violent periods in its history, becoming a target of not only neighboring Muslim empires but also Christian Europeans who campaigned into the Levant and North Africa during the Crusades.

A war-torn Egypt emerged in the late medieval times before it was ultimately conquered in the 16th century by the Ottoman Empire, which imposed its rule on Egypt for the next three centuries. During the 19th century, amidst massive global sociopolitical, technological, and economic transformations, Egypt came to be dominated by the British Empire. British colonialism left a rather painful mark on Egypt, but it was the beginning of a period when much of Egypt's past was rediscovered.

Finally, after years of struggle, Egypt emerged as an independent nation. Almost instantly, it began to play an increasing role in the regional political landscape, something that still stands true to this day. As modern Egypt tries to navigate through the turbulent times of the 21st century, it has to confront many domestic and foreign challenges.

This book will tell the long and compelling history of Egypt. The opening chapters of the book are concerned with the rise of the ancient Egyptian civilization. It will examine how ancient Egypt came to be and focus on the most prevalent figures and events that shaped ancient Egypt and our understanding of it. The ancient period is extensive and complicated, as it is full of mystery and open to different interpretations. The middle part of the book will cover the transition of Egypt from ancient to medieval times, starting with the spread of Islam and subsequent cultural transformations. These chapters will focus on the emergence of local Egyptian empires during the medieval era, which became regional powerhouses and vied for dominance against numerous adversaries for many centuries.

The history of medieval Egypt ends with its conquest by the Ottoman Empire, which ushered in a three-century-long period of great social and political change as the world began to slowly modernize. The final chapters of the book will accompany Egypt from the end of the Ottoman rule in Egypt through its colonization by the British and its independence in the 20th century. This part of the book will highlight some of the key social and cultural conflicts that emerged during this time, which ultimately contributed to the development of a unique national identity in Egypt and the formation of a modern state. Surveying Egypt in the 20th century means taking a look at the ambitious personalities that shaped the country and helped it navigate through the globalized modern world.

Chapter One – The Origins of Egypt

Predynastic Egypt and Unification

Humans had long inhabited the great Nile River Valley, a narrow stretch of land a few thousand kilometers long. The river was a beacon of life amidst the vast deserts of North Africa, which were filled with barren wastelands of sand and rock. Here, the Egyptian civilization emerged in the late 4th millennium BCE. Before then, a couple of early Neolithic cultures sprang up along almost the entire length of the river and by its delta in the north. Though we have no textual evidence of these cultures, archaeological findings have identified two of the most prominent cultures that preceded the early dynastic developments in the late 4th millennium BCE.

The Badarian culture, which archaeologists suggest existed roughly between 4400 and 4000 BCE, was most likely the earliest that practiced agriculture in Upper Egypt (the southern regions of the Nile; the Nile flows south to north). The Badarian way of life was very primitive and based on subsistence farming of crops like wheat and barley.

The Badarian culture was succeeded by the Naqada culture, which is divided into three periods (I-III) and lasted roughly until 3200 BCE. These periods were similar in their social and cultural characteristics to the Badarian culture and provided the foundations upon which the ancient Egyptian civilization would be built. During the Naqada III phase, we can observe the beginnings of territorial or political unification of parts of Egypt, with evidence of burial sites of kings that preceded the First Dynasty. The existence of different types of burial sites, which contain luxurious materials like gold and lapis lazuli, suggests that a certain kind of hierarchical distinction already existed during the late 4th millennium BCE. In fact, the ancient name of Naqada was Nubt, which means the "city of gold" due to its proximity to the eastern desert territories where gold was in abundance. Again, the core centers of the late Naqada culture were concentrated in Upper Egypt but gradually began to spread toward Lower Egypt in the north. This was most likely because the people wanted access to the Mediterranean trade routes, which had been gradually developing over the years. We know that these cultures were part of the extensive ancient trade network; the discovery of lapis lazuli, for example, which could have only come from central Asia, is a testament to this fact.

Around 3000 BCE, there is evidence of the rapid development of the civilization that would eventually become ancient Egypt. Archaeological findings of this era, such as the use of sun-dried bricks and pottery styles from Mesopotamia, suggest more contact with neighboring civilizations and cultures. The predynastic cultures developed a unique sense of identity despite the obvious influence of Mesopotamian societies.

Around this time, the unification process of Upper and Lower Egypt had begun, though there still persists a debate on who exactly was the first king of a unified Egypt. Later tradition would reveal the existence of a legendary king by the name of Menes, who founded Memphis—the future capital of Egypt—and brought enlightenment to his people. Menes is recognized by a 3rd-century-BCE Egyptian historian, Manetho, as the first king. Herodotus, the "father of history," called the legendary king by his Greek name, Min.

What is certainly puzzling with Menes is the fact that little to no archaeological evidence survives that points to his existence. According to some traditions, he is a descendant of the god Horus, who, according to mythology, was the first pharaoh. This phenomenon is common among ancient civilizations. It served as a way of legitimizing the leader, be it a king or a religious figure like a priest. Nowadays, most historians and Egyptologists believe Menes to have been the same person as Narmer, the pharaoh who is credited with the unification of Upper and Lower Egypt and the founding of the First Dynasty.

Unlike Menes, Narmer, whose name is spelled with the hieroglyphs for "catfish" and "chisel," survives in archaeological evidence. He is thought to be depicted as the unifier of Upper and Lower Egypt in the famous Narmer Palette, a cosmetic palette that was discovered in the late 19th century at the site of Hierakonpolis. On the palette, he is shown wearing the traditional crowns of the two regions: the *hedjet* or white crown, a symbol of Upper Egypt, and the *deshret* or red crown for Lower Egypt. Another archaeological find, the Narmer mace head, depicts the seated king receiving what appears to be captives and booty as a gift, reinforcing the idea that he was a real person.

The Narmer Palette.[1]

What causes confusion with regard to the historical identities of Narmer and Menes is the fact that Narmer is the *serekh* name (a royal title), whereas Menes appears to be a personal name. We can deduce this by the fact that the royal annals from later periods, mostly the New Kingdom period, contain the personal names of the pharaohs of unified Egypt, and they begin with Menes. Taking this all into consideration, it is likely that Menes and Narmer refer to the same semi-mythical figure who is believed to be the first unifier of Upper and Lower Egypt and the founder of the First Dynasty.

Narmer unified Upper and Lower Egypt sometime during the late 4th century, between 3200 and 3000 BCE. The foundations for a unified proto-state had already been provided by the latest Naqada rulers, as they had extended their administration to include both parts of the region. By this time, the two centers of the two regions had emerged, having developed somewhat distinct functions that would last well into the next centuries. Hierakonpolis, the city that we mentioned above, became an important center in the north for the worship of the god Horus. He was associated with the sky and symbolized the living king. In the south, a similar role was assumed by Abydos, which served as a center for the cult of the dead king. It was also one of the earliest places where political power was concentrated.

While it is difficult to assume how exactly the unification of Upper and Lower Egypt took place, it was likely through military conflict. The Narmer Palette illustrates dead enemies by King Narmer. During the 20th century, an alternative interpretation suggested that the sudden emergence of the culturally distinct features of the dynastic Egyptian civilization from the Naqada culture was the result of a forceful foreign imposition. However, this theory has been dismissed. Despite this, there is considerable evidence that the predynastic cultures in Egypt were contacting societies in the Levant, as demonstrated by the discovery of an abundance of Egyptian pottery in the Sinai region.

Early Ancient Egyptians

Ancient Egyptian society was concentrated around the notion of kingship, something that was of great importance to the Egyptians. The king was believed to have been the reincarnation of the god Horus and was seen to be an exalted, omnipotent figure. As we mentioned, during the early days of ancient Egypt, the king derived part of his legitimacy from controlling both Upper and Lower Egypt. It was thought that the divine order was maintained if the two parts were unified, and early Egyptian kings had a distinct title to emphasize the fact that they ruled over both the north and the south. The name "Two Lands" signifies that the two regions that made up Egypt were different enough to have their own social identities. However, it also suggests that Upper and Lower Egypt shared many characteristics that could have been deemed Egyptian as early as the late 4th millennium BCE.

Naturally, the king oversaw the political and administrative system of early ancient Egypt in addition to serving as its spiritual leader. He was seen to be the closest to the deities. During the early days of Egyptian state-building, the king's servants who ruled over the different towns or regions of the kingdom were usually his kinsmen. Eventually, this system led to the emergence of the nomes, the ancient Egyptian administrative divisions that were ruled by a nomarch. Much of the history of ancient Egypt was marked by power struggles between the king and the nomarchs, who would sometimes manage to accrue enough regional power to eclipse the ruler's might. The relationships that developed between the different nomes and their nomarchs in relation to the king were very complex and diverse, further contributing to the emergence of distinct regional identities throughout Egypt.

We don't really know for sure the extent of the territories directly ruled by ancient Egyptian kings, as state and regional boundaries were not clearly fixed then. There was virtually unrestricted inter-regional access through the many ancient trade routes, and we can only identify the extent of the influence of the Egyptian culture through archaeological findings. It certainly stretched east of the Nile into the mountainous regions through to the Red Sea as early as the reign of King Narmer before 3000 BCE. During the reign of his successor, Aha (c. 3000-2970 BCE), contact with the Sinai Peninsula and Palestine became more apparent. The Levant supplied Egypt with valuable timber, which was always in great demand in the desert. The trade relationships between Egypt and the Levant and even beyond to Mesopotamia developed during prehistoric times and continued to shape ancient Egyptian history for many centuries.

King Narmer or Menes is considered to be the founder of the First Dynasty. He is credited with shifting the political center of Egypt to the north in Memphis, which gradually grew in importance. It was located at a strategic position near the southern tip of the Nile Delta. Abydos, in the south, was a religious center where King Aha and other kings of the First Dynasty built large royal tombs for themselves and members of their families. Interestingly, Aha was probably the first king to begin working on the Saqqara necropolis in Upper Egypt, close to Memphis. Constructed from dried mudbricks and partially built into the rock, the first of the northern tombs contained subterranean chambers.

Over time, a tradition of burying royal officials at Saqqara developed, and the site grew into a full-on necropolis. Some of the tombs have survived the test of time. While the occupants of most of the tombs and their respective years of construction have been identified, the site was a frequent target for thieves and robbers. This means that much of the material evidence, such as valuables, tablets, weapons, and jewelry, which were intended to accompany the dead in the afterlife, was stolen. In fact, archaeologists rarely discovered royal tombs that were completely intact.

Such an occurrence rightfully attracted a lot of attention.

The formation of a unified Egyptian state also brought about a period of innovation that transformed the makeup of Egyptian society. Progress meant the need for order to better integrate the growing society. A unified system of dating was adopted sometime around King Aha's reign, which divided the calendar year into three seasons with four months of thirty days. There were also five additional seasonal days that increased the total number of days to 365, making it very close to the Julian calendar, which was used by the Western world for a long time. Individual years began to be named after important events that took place during that year. For example, in the year of the "Visit," the king visited a sanctuary at Neith. Names of the years were, of course, royally issued and are present in the tablets that contain the royal annals.

Another important development around this time was the Egyptian writing system, which was invented before the First Dynasty rose to power. The ancient Egyptian hieroglyphic system is not a pure alphabet in the sense that each sign can be interpreted in different ways depending on the whole text and the context in which it is used. Most of the signs are depictions of real or abstract objects and represent a sequence of consonants that indicate not only the object that is represented but also the pronunciation of the word for the object in ancient Egyptian. Hieroglyphs were deciphered in the 19th century after the discovery of arguably the most important archaeological discoveries ever, the Rosetta Stone, a tablet that contained a royal decree from the 2nd century BCE inscribed in Egyptian hieroglyphs, Demotic, and ancient Greek.

Ancient Greek is our best tool for analyzing the ancient Egyptian language and learning about hieroglyphs. We know the pronunciations of the vowels in the Coptic language, which is the latest stage of development of ancient Egyptian and is still spoken to some extent in the liturgies of the Coptic Orthodox Church, which was founded in the 1st century CE. Many royal names were transcribed throughout the centuries and are sometimes based on foreign linguistic influences. In addition to the hieroglyphic script, there was an ancient Egyptian cursive writing style, hieratic, which was mainly used until the middle of the 1st millennium BCE. It gave rise to the Demotic script, which became the prominent way of writing from around 650 BCE.

The First and Second Dynasties

King Aha was succeeded in the early 3rd millennium BCE by King Djer. Our knowledge of his reign is limited and laced with semi-legendary and mythological accounts. For instance, his tomb, located at the royal cemetery in Abydos, was thought to have been the tomb of Osiris, a leading deity in the Egyptian pantheon. Djer is mentioned in several of the most prominent royal king lists, which mention that he ruled for up to fifty years.

After him came King Djet, whose name means "Serpent of Horus." He most likely ruled for the next ten years during the 30th century BCE. Djet prominently figures in ancient Egyptian sources, and his tomb stela, preserved in pristine condition and bearing the Horus name of the pharaoh, is now in the Louvre Museum. We can assume that his consort, Queen Merneith, was also a figure of great importance during Djet's reign, signified by the existence of her tombs in both Abydos and Saqqara. This is interesting, considering the fact that she bore no royal titles. She might have ruled as a regent before Djet's heir and her son, Den, came of age. Merneith is one of the earliest prominent female rulers of Egypt. Generally, women were highly respected in ancient Egyptian society and had extensive legal rights.

King Den (or Dewen) ruled Egypt after Djer, ascending the throne between 2900 and 2880 BCE.[1] Compared to other rulers of the First Dynasty, Den has far more archaeological evidence to attest to his reign. The abundance of such evidence has led many to suppose that Egypt experienced a period of prosperity and stability during King Den's reign, which lasted for about four decades.

Fragments from the Palermo Stone and the Cairo Stone mention events that took place during this time by providing names for the different regnal years. We can assume that Egypt went to war with the neighboring peoples during the middle of his reign, in the nineteenth and twenty-first regnal years, something that can be attested from the inscriptions that mention "Smiting of the East." His tomb in Abydos features a floor made out of red granite and diorite stelae that also depict

---

[1] There is no way to know the exact dates of the earliest rulers and developments in ancient Egypt. The regnal years often differ based on the chronologies used by historians. New research and evidence also affect this. For instance, recent radiocarbon data fixes the years of his reign to between 3011 and 2921 BCE.

the king, who is wearing the double crown, hinting at the fact that he was the king of Upper and Lower Egypt.

The First Dynasty appears to have entered a period of decline after Den's reign. The reigns of the last three kings of this dynasty were marked by political instability, resulting in the temporary abandonment of Abydos as a royal cemetery around 2800 BCE. Perhaps this signifies the decline of the historically prominent Upper Egypt region and the rise in the political dominance of Lower Egypt, with new sections constructed at the royal residence in Memphis and Saqqara.

King Ninetjer was likely the third pharaoh of the Second Dynasty in the 28th century BCE. Our knowledge of Egypt after him is very limited, with some annals pointing to the existence of two rulers at the same time. What we do know about Ninetjer is that he ruled for about forty years and that he was probably celebrated by festivals like Sed, a ceremony that served to symbolically "renew" the pharaoh's reign after he had ruled for about thirty years. The small statuette of Ninetjer that has been discovered most likely depicts the king wearing special attire that was worn by the pharaohs during the Sed festival. The creation of a king's statue would eventually become a tradition of the Sed festival, a staple of Egyptian monarchs during the later dynasties. It symbolized the "burial" of the "old" king in the statue after many years of rule, during which he was believed to have exhausted his spiritual capabilities, leading to the rebirth of the new king.

State unity was under threat after the end of Ninetjer's rule. The next few pharaohs were not attested in Upper and Lower Egypt, and some of them were omitted from the king lists created during the later periods. These kings either did not enjoy widespread popularity during their lifetimes or their reigns were denounced later on. King Hudjefa, for example, whose name literally translates to "missing" and features in the Turin King List, which was compiled around 1245 BCE, might not have existed at all. Egypt might have had no king during this time.

We can also assume that the ambiguity of the pharaohs from this period was caused by a shift in the conception of kingship, which might have arisen from regional differences. One of the Second Dynasty kings, for example, bears the serekh name of Seth-Peribsen, indicating the importance bestowed on the god Seth, the god of deserts and violence. As we mentioned, the god-king Horus was associated with Egyptian kingship by this time, so the use of Seth's name might suggest a temporary break from tradition. This break might have been caused by instability or turmoil. Around the same time, the royal cemetery at Abydos was reinstated, suggesting a greater importance of Upper Egypt during Seth-Peribsen's reign and the rise of the cult of Seth in the south.

The last ruler of the Second Dynasty was Khasekhemwy, who ascended the throne in around 2690 and ruled for about twenty years. State unity was restored during his reign, mostly through a series of successful military campaigns. Interestingly, the pharaoh's serekh name bears the symbols for both Horus and Seth, pointing to unification. It is possible that he defeated Seth-Peribsen in a civil war, though this theory has little evidence. In addition to his campaigns, Khasekhemwy is known for his many building projects. These structures are important due to the increasing use of stone as a prominent material. Techniques used in Egyptian architecture eventually produced the many famous pyramids during the Old Kingdom. Khasekhemwy's reign brought stability back to the realm and brought about one of the most important periods in Egyptian history: the Third Dynasty.

Chapter Two – The Old Kingdom

The Old Kingdom is one of the most important and iconic periods in ancient Egyptian history. This is true despite the fact that for the ancient Egyptians themselves, the transition between the Early Dynastic and Old Kingdom periods was most likely not that clear. For us, however, the Old Kingdom is marked by remarkable political developments, which led to Egypt becoming one of the most advanced civilizations in the ancient world. Importantly, this era, which lasted from around 2700 to 2150 BCE, introduced new elements in other aspects of life, such as culture. During the Old Kingdom, Egyptian pharaohs perfected the craft of pyramid-building, erecting some of the most magnificent structures of the ancient era. Let's take a look at the major developments during this roughly six-hundred-year history, as well as the brief First Intermediate Period, which can be considered the first major crisis in Egyptian history.

Djoser

The Old Kingdom is thought to have been founded around 2691 BCE, which was the year King Djoser, who is often referred to as the first ruler of the Third Dynasty of Egypt, took the throne. Our understanding and dating of ancient Egyptian periods largely stem from the already existing nomenclature of ancient historians and chroniclers. The classification of Egypt's kings in the dynasties was introduced by a 3rd-century BCE historian, Manetho. What we do know about this time in Egyptian history is that it was incredibly prosperous, leading to domestic stability and political dominance. During the Old Kingdom, the Egyptian political system became increasingly centralized, and even greater importance was attributed to the pharaoh, who stood at the heart of it.

While a lot is known about King Djoser's reign, historians are less sure when it comes to accurately dating his tenure as king. He was most likely the son of King Khasekhemwy and Queen Nimaathap. However, there are questions regarding whether or not he was the legitimate and designated heir to the throne. Interestingly, in certain Egyptian king lists, King Nebka is considered to be the founder of the Third Dynasty, though this is contested. As one can already observe, the main problem about this period is the dating, which can cause a lot of confusion. Fortunately, we do have solid archaeological evidence from the Old Kingdom that shows Egyptian cultural and political practices developed during this time, differentiating it from the rule of the preceding dynasties.

The Old Kingdom rulers are best known for their large-scale building projects. Djoser's Step Pyramid, located at the Saqqara necropolis, is a monument that reinforces the great standing of the pharaoh. The name Djoser translates to "sacred" or "holy." Standing at 62.5 meters tall with a 121-meter by 109-meter base, the pyramid is considered to be one of the earliest large-scale stone monuments in the world. Before its construction, stone was used in a limited way in Egyptian or ancient building projects in general. The royal tombs constructed during the Early Dynastic Period, for example, were built with brick. Djoser's pyramid is a six-step structure, and it initially had the design of a mastaba, a rectangular flat-roofed tomb with inclined sides, which was the go-to style for earlier tombs.

Pyramid of Djoser taken in 1916.[2]

The pyramid is surrounded by an enclosure of what most likely was a demarcation to distinguish the pharaoh's tomb from the rest of the tombs at the necropolis. Beside it are several structures, most likely shrines, with stone decorations that might have been used to celebrate the pharaoh's Sed festival. The mastermind behind the structure was Imhotep, who is often credited as being the inventor of stone-building techniques. His name is inscribed at the base of Djoser's statue, and he was considered to have been such an important figure that he was later deified as the son of the god Ptah, the patron of architects. In addition to being the most important architect of ancient Egypt, Imhotep was also a high priest of Heliopolis, one of the oldest Lower Egyptian cities. Though Imhotep's tomb has not yet been identified, it is probable that it was located near Djoser's pyramid, perhaps somewhere inside the enclosure.

Djoser's pyramid is the earliest example of the grandiose royal tombs that would become a staple of the Old Kingdom dynasties. The design was adopted to reflect the divine, exalted status of the pharaoh in Egyptian society.

Construction of such a structure was difficult. The next few attempts at constructing such structures by Djoser's successors ended in failure. For instance, the Pyramid of Sekhemkhet, located southwest of Djoser's pyramid, was never completed. The fact that the project was abandoned is signified by the existence of an underground burial chamber with an empty sarcophagus. The pyramid of King Khaba, the third king of the Third Dynasty, was also probably abandoned during construction. The reason behind this might have been the relatively short reigns of the two pharaohs. Nevertheless, important groundwork for constructing the pyramids had been laid. The techniques would be advanced in later years and would eventually usher in the rather short-lived Age of Pyramids.

The Fourth Dynasty and the Age of Pyramids

The Fourth Dynasty played an immense role in shaping ancient Egyptian society and culture. Beginning with the long reign of King Sneferu (c. 2613–2589 BCE), pyramid-building methods reached new heights. Three pyramids were constructed during Sneferu's reign, two of which, the Bent Pyramid and the Red Pyramid, are located at the site of Dahshur, which became a pyramid complex. A certain consistency in their designs and layouts emerged, something that likely was associated with profound cultural changes that elevated the position of the sun god Ra.

The Bent Pyramid is an interesting limestone structure that derives its name from the altered angles of the sloping sides, which were modified sometime during the early stages of construction, most likely after the discovery of a flaw in the pyramid's design. This gives the pyramid a distinct rhomboid shape, and it has a remarkable height of about one hundred meters. The Red Pyramid, named after the red-colored limestone that was used to build it, is located to the north. It is the largest of the pyramids in the complex. It also serves as the burial site of King Sneferu. The third pyramid attributed to Sneferu is located at Meidum in Lower Egypt. The pyramid might have actually been built during the reigns of one of Sneferu's predecessors.

The main criterion for distinguishing the Fourth Dynasty from the Third Dynasty is the architectural style of the pyramids. During the reign of Khufu (c. 2589-2566 BCE), such techniques were perfected, leading to the construction of the famous Great Pyramid of Giza, the only surviving ancient world wonders. Khufu, who was given the name Cheops by Herodotus, is a somewhat insignificant ruler aside from the Great Pyramid. The pyramid reached a height of 146.5 meters with a ground base of 230 square meters. The Great Pyramid of Khufu was the largest pyramid made in Egypt. It had a unique design that placed the royal burial chamber at the center of the structure instead of at below ground level. Notoriously built from more than two million building blocks, many of which weighed several tons, the Great Pyramid featured a white limestone casing, which was removed over the years to give the pyramid the distinct look that it has today.

Although Khufu's body and the funerary equipment that would follow him to the afterlife should have been in the pyramid, no actual remains were recovered during the pyramid's excavations. Most likely, the pyramid was looted by robbers. Importantly, three smaller pyramids were constructed by Khufu for his queens, located to the east of the pharaoh's tomb. These structures, however, just like the rest of the pyramids at the Giza pyramid complex, are overshadowed by the sheer magnificence of the Great Pyramid. The architect behind the structure was the vizier of King Khufu, Hemiunu, whose mastaba is located near the pharaoh's tomb in the cemetery west of the Great Pyramid.

Khufu had many sons, which complicated the matter of succession. Djedefra was probably the son of Khufu from a lesser queen and ruled until around 2558 BCE. Archaeological excavations suggest that he began building two pyramids, neither of which were completed. He was succeeded by his brother, Khafre, also known by his Greek name Chephren. He and his son, Menkaure, built the other two pyramids at Giza, which are smaller compared to the Great Pyramid. Interestingly, the design of Khafre's pyramid, which originally reached about 146 meters in height and now stands at about 136 meters, makes it seem as if it was intended to be viewed as equal in status to Khufu's pyramid.

The Giza pyramid complex.[3]

Khafre constructed more than just his pyramid at Giza. He erected a grand guardian statue located north of the valley temple that eventually led to his pyramid. The Great Sphinx is a statue of a human-headed lion that measures about seventy-two meters long and twenty meters tall. During the late years of ancient Egypt, it was worshiped in its own right as a statue dedicated to Horus. The Sphinx was only recently excavated in the 20th century to reveal its huge lion body, which had previously been covered with sand. Needless to say, it has become one of the most unique monuments around the world.

Egyptian Society during the Old Kingdom

The transition from mostly mudbrick structures, such as simple mastabas, into large monuments like the pyramids was a huge technological step that should be analyzed in relation to the broader cultural and social developments in Egypt. One such development concerned the notion of kingship. In virtually any ancient civilization, power and influence were concentrated in the hands of different types of people. Some societies had been united around prominent military leaders who had managed to impose their dominance on neighboring or rival tribes or factions. In other societies, the religious class occupied the chief role in the hierarchy, shaping the beliefs of the people and playing a big role when it came to the emergence of certain values regarding different moral issues.

As a mediator between the gods and the people, Egyptian pharaohs naturally enjoyed a special position. There have been many instances throughout history when the king was believed to possess divine attributes or even acted as the representative of the gods on earth. There is evidence of this in both Western and Eastern traditions. The pharaoh was the manifestation of the hawk god Horus and the two goddesses Nekhbet and Wadjet, the latter of which represented the "two lands" of Egypt. It was believed that after the death of the king, he moved on to the afterlife, where he was accepted by the gods.

This was why religious rituals, including burial rites and other ceremonies, were of paramount importance for the ancient Egyptians. Kings were buried with a whole range of different objects. People believed that the most important objects were necessary for the king, as they would follow him into his afterlife, guaranteeing his well-being. This was also true for the king's closest allies and subordinates, who would be buried in the vicinity of his tomb so they could accompany him to the afterlife. The extensive building activities of the kings of the Fourth Dynasty and beyond included burial sites for the king's relatives, viziers, and friends. Although these tombs were far simpler mastabas that were mostly constructed of mudbricks, their precise placement in burial complexes granted each a symbolic importance and resulted in the development of advanced complexes. Of course, the main tomb—that of the king—occupied a central position in the complex.

The development of the pyramid tombs was in the common interests of the Egyptian people. It was a better way to safeguard the king's journey to the afterlife, and the pyramids also expressed the magnanimity and status of the monarch. The pyramids were a manifestation of the king's authority through their sheer scale. Due to their symbolic and cultural significance, the pyramid complexes were protected by royal decrees, and special personnel were assigned to keep watch over them. This led to the development of cults of the deceased kings, which assumed a special place in the hierarchy of Egyptian beliefs and led to the establishment of regional cults.

It is important to also point out here that a lot more importance was devoted to aesthetics once pyramids became the staple for royal tombs. The Old Kingdom saw the advancement of arts and crafts, such as the carving of reliefs on the facades of important buildings. Relief carving was crucial for further developing stone-cutting and refining techniques, which indirectly resulted in the creation of many large-scale statues of pharaohs and deities. Statues that depicted the kings were often placed in burial chambers, symbolizing the soul (*ka*) of the pharaohs. Statues of Djoser and Khafre are among the most prominent examples of early Old Kingdom styles, and these styles would be further advanced as the centuries passed.

Large-scale building projects, such as pyramids, were only possible because of the relative stability and economic prosperity that Egypt enjoyed during the Old Kingdom period. For instance, the creation of a pyramid required the mobilization of a previously unseen number of workers. Tens of thousands of people were involved in the construction of pyramids and the burial complexes around them. They were involved in not only the building but also the logistics of the projects, such as planning, the maintenance of the sites, and transporting materials.

The ancient Egyptian economy and society were not as dependent on slave labor as one might suppose. Instead, most of the workforce, when it came to pyramid-building, was made up of individuals from different fields of the economy, including agriculture, which was of pivotal importance in ancient Egypt. In order to combat the alterations in the volume and intensity of agricultural production and to avoid disruptions of food supplies throughout the state, effective measures had to be introduced by the government. The state had to make sure to redistribute supplies to those regions that might have been deprived of laborers, something that was made possible because of the centralized nature of the ancient Egyptian political system.

During the Old Kingdom, the kings undertook the first significant administrative reforms that would shape Egypt for centuries to come. The administrative centers of different regions, or nomes (existing royal estates or towns where a large number of people was concentrated) emerged as places from which surrounding areas could be locally governed. The nomes gained more and more importance over time, thanks to the fact they were the centers of tax collection in ancient Egypt. The local governors sent the revenue to the capital, the seat of the pharaoh. The king, who had virtually absolute authority to impose taxes and distribute lands, could exercise his authority to a certain extent throughout the vast lands of his kingdom. An effective bureaucracy was needed to make sure that the state ran smoothly, and delegating certain responsibilities to the nomarchs was one solution. During the early days of this administrative system, people closest to the pharaohs were usually appointed to rule as nomarchs.

Economic growth reached a new high during the Old Kingdom. One factor behind this was the way the state exercised its authority over the provinces and collected revenue. Another reason was the development of new trade routes, which were perhaps started to accommodate the newly emerging demands for different materials associated with the construction of pyramids. The inscriptions of Egyptian kings' names in distant territories are a testament to the extent of their influence and (partial) presence. There is evidence of these inscriptions scattered around the Sinai Peninsula and the Nubian desert quarries, some sixty to seventy kilometers to the west of the territories controlled by Egypt at the time.

The Egyptian state was also stable during the Old Kingdom because of the absence of a major external threat, thanks to, in part, the extensive military campaigns in neighboring territories. These are attested to in later inscriptions, such as the Palermo Stone, created during the Fifth Dynasty around 2340 BCE. King Sneferu, for example, sent an expedition to Nubia, securing several thousand heads of cattle, as well as human captives, which were added to the existing slave labor system.

Fifth and Sixth Dynasties

With the accession of Userkaf in around 2494 BCE, the Fifth Dynasty began. This dynasty would see the development of new cult beliefs centered around the son god Ra. Nowadays, Ra is one of the most widely known deities from ancient Egyptian mythology.

Interestingly, we know very little about the reign of Userkaf. The main evidence that survives from his short, about seven-year, tenure as king is the temple building dedicated to Ra at Abusir, north of Saqqara. This set off a trend for the remainder of the Fifth Dynasty kings, who put their efforts into constructing temples dedicated to Ra instead of pyramids that would be on a similar scale as those during the earlier dynasties. Userkaf's pyramid survives. It is located in northern Saqqara, though it is by no means as advanced and complete as the ones we discussed earlier. All in all, the designs of the sun temples closely resemble those of the pyramid complexes, proven by the existence of causeways that connect the important parts of the buildings with each other. It is not unlikely that Ra was elevated to the position of a chief state deity for the first time during the Fifth Dynasty. On the other hand, the intricate designs of the sun temples suggest the willingness of the kings to connect themselves personally with Ra, cultivating a "relationship" with the deity that would last into their afterlife.

It is important to remember that the Old Kingdom was still at an early stage in the development of Egyptian society and culture. During this time, the Egyptian belief system, though being, generally speaking, consistent, was regionally diverse, with each city having its own chief deity and distinct identity. The importance of some deities, such as Horus, was universally recognized. Nevertheless, the Fifth Dynasty kings took care of regional beliefs and respected the deities worshiped in different parts of Egypt. They made donations to their temples and helped when it came to a temple's maintenance. This could explain the increase in the number of religious and state officials who were buried in specially designed tombs. The mastaba of Ti (Ty), located at Saqqara, is considered to be one of the most important archaeological discoveries of the Old Kingdom period. Belonging to Ti, a state official and architect of several sun temples, the mastaba contains several statues and relief carvings that were previously only observed in royal tombs.

An even more significant legacy of the Fifth Dynasty was the institution of a practice that became customary for royal tombs in the future. The pyramid of King Unas (r. c. 2375-2345 BCE), located at the southeastern part of Djoser's enclosure in northern Saqqara, contains the earliest evidence of the Pyramid Texts, which were inscribed on the walls of the royal burial chamber. The contents of these inscriptions are compelling. Most of the texts describe rituals, rites, and ceremonies that were supposed to help the king get to the afterlife. Many of the texts are hymns or spells whose function was to protect the king's journey to the afterlife. They were supposed to be chanted during the different rituals associated with burial. Some of the texts are personal; they sometimes depict the life of the king and praise his achievements. The Pyramid Texts also reveal the increasing importance bestowed upon Osiris, the Egyptian god of agriculture who was ultimately elevated to the position of the overseer of the afterlife and the judge of the dead.

The reign of Unas marks the end of the Fifth Dynasty. His successor, Teti (c. 2345-2323 BCE), is considered to be the first pharaoh of the Sixth Dynasty. Teti was indirectly related to his predecessor; his wife, Iput, was the daughter of Unas. The ambiguity of the different sources about the transition of power from Unas to Teti suggests a potential succession struggle. The change in dynasty most likely caused a change in the royal residence, though the tombs of the Sixth Dynasty are still located at Saqqara. The small pyramid of Teti at Saqqara is surrounded by tombs of relatives and important members of the royal administration, such as that of Mereruka, a royal vizier. Mereruka's tomb has an impressively decorated thirty-two chambers, suggesting the importance of his position during Teti's reign.

Teti was succeeded by King Pepi (Pepy) I (c. 2321–2287 BCE), who is a peculiar character because he changed his regnal name several times during his lifetime. The accession of Pepi I and his reign marks the appearance of the first cracks in the supremacy of the notion of Egyptian kingship. Contemporary sources reveal that the king was subject to a conspiracy that had emerged from complications in the royal harem. In the later years of his reign, Pepi married the two daughters of an Upper Egypt nomarch, Khui, who had his residence at Abydos. This signifies the increasing power of local rulers, especially those in Upper Egypt, who were farther away from the capital. The increased power of local rulers is attested to by the organization of several state-endorsed but locally planned expeditions into foreign territories to tap into the trade and resources of neighboring areas. Royal inscriptions and the Pyramid Texts reveal that these campaigns were largely successful, contributing to the regional hegemony of ancient Egypt.

Perhaps the most intriguing reign of the late Old Kingdom was King Pepi II Neferkare, which, according to Manetho, lasted for about ninety-four years, from circa 2270 to 2205 BCE. This is partially reconfirmed by the Turin King List, which was compiled in the 13th century BCE during the New Kingdom. If this is true, it makes Pepi II the longest-reigning monarch in all of human history, though, of course, we don't know for sure if it is true. In any case, Pepi II likely succeeded the throne at a very young age and probably outlived most of his viziers, advisors, and members of his family. His accession to the throne at a young age is attested to by the discovery of an alabaster statuette depicting the young king seated in the lap of his mother, Queen Ankhesenmeryre II, who probably acted as a regent before Pepi II came of age.

There are several ways to interpret the unusually long reigns of kings. The length of the reign, of course, depends on the good health of the monarch, but it also points to stability and relative prosperity. However, long reigns tend to lead to a period of destabilization after the death of the monarch, who would have emerged as a symbol of rulership and safety. The decline of the Old Kingdom occurred less than a decade after the death of Pepi II. Contemporary evidence suggests that Egyptian expeditions to neighboring foreign lands continued to the same extent, and no significant actor threatened the safety of the kingdom during this time. Instead, an array of domestic difficulties snowballed into the decline of the power and influence of the centralized political system.

Pepi II's loss of authority was partially caused by the fact that he was young when he ascended the throne, making him incapable of ruling. The regent queen enjoyed the status of being regent, which is attested to by the discovery of her lavish pyramid, which bears the evidence for the earliest Pyramid Text inscriptions made for a queen. Some historians argue that this resulted in Pepi II being influenced by his mother and her family's faction even once he became an adult.

However, the gradual decline of monarchical authority was caused by other factors, such as the increase in the number of local cults. These movements developed distinct regional identities, which undermined the unity of the kingdom and rendered the king powerless vis-à-vis the nomarchs. Pepi II, as well as several other kings before him, failed to provide for the changing political circumstances that threatened their own positions.

As the institution of the nomarchs grew in size and legitimacy, nomarchs were no longer allies or relatives of the pharaoh. Instead, they established regional hereditary "dynasties," thus weakening the state's reach and involvement in their activities. As a consequence, the flow of money into the state treasury gradually decreased. The lack of resources meant that the king could not enforce his authority because he could no longer muster up a large enough army to overpower the forces assembled by the nomarchs. The nomarchs began to increasingly defy the central authority after the death of Pepi II in around 2205 BCE.

First Intermediate Period

Pepi II's son, Merenre, was very old when he ascended the throne. His reign only lasted for just over a year. Several sources, including the Turn King List, Manetho, and Herodotus, agree on the fact that he was followed by a succession of kings whose reigns were also short. However, the almost two-hundred-year-long period, beginning from roughly the end of Pepi II's reign up until around 2055 BCE under King Mentuhotep II, was an era of instability and uncertainty in ancient Egypt.

Known as the First Intermediate Period, this time can be considered the first instance of a long-term crisis in ancient Egyptian history. The period was marked by the radical decline of the king's power. The king still resided in Memphis but was only nominally in charge of the state because of the growing influence of regional nomarchs. This led to chaos and confusion in Egypt. Manetho mentions that there were seventy different kings in Memphis during this period, each ruling for a period of just one day.

The rulers of the Seventh and Eighth Dynasties only effectively ruled over Memphis and its surrounding areas at best. Not much is known about the nature of their reigns, and it is even difficult to say which of the kings mentioned in the sources truly existed and which did not. It is not entirely improbable that a network of powerful nomarchs intentionally carved up Upper and Lower Egypt among themselves in a sort of oligarchic system.

The decline of kingly authority meant the decline of the influence of Memphis. Other cities rose to prominence, like Heracleopolis (not to be confused with Hierakonpolis), which began to eclipse Memphis as the principal city in Lower Egypt. The kings of the Ninth and Tenth Dynasties I were originally nomarchs of Heracleopolis, though the extent of their power, especially to the south, is unclear. A similar development took place in Upper Egypt, where the city of Thebes emerged as an important political center and began to grow in size during the First Intermediate Period. Theban rulers gave rise to the Eleventh Dynasty, which began around 2150. A member of this line would finally unite Egypt in the mid-21st century BCE.

The two factions became natural rivals and claimed legitimacy and the title of the pharaoh throughout the First Intermediate Period. They wrestled each other for influence over the other nomes for about a century, with neither managing to gain the upper hand. Little detailed archaeological evidence survives from this era, and the lack of primary sources is a testament to the instability and chaos Egypt faced.

An interesting piece of evidence that refers to the crisis of the First Intermediate Period is the Ipuwer Papyrus, a poem originally composed in the 20th century BCE that describes the troubles Egypt suffered during the time. Only a 13th-century BCE copy of the poem survives today. It is a typical example of the pessimistic artistic genre that became popular during the Middle Kingdom, the era that followed the First Intermediate

Period. The text hints at the lawlessness that was present in Egypt, and its author longs for the return of the older days, which were filled with stability and predictability.

Intef the Elder is considered to be the founder of the Eleventh Dynasty, which originated in Thebes. He was most likely the nomarch of Thebes at a time when it began to grow its influence. His importance as the founder of the Theban dynasty is referred to in later inscriptions. His successors began to take the fight to the north and claim suzerainty and legitimacy as the king of all Egypt, though this was only achieved around 2050 BCE. One of the most contested places between the two factions was the city of Abydos, which quickly grew as a religious center of Egypt. It was centered around the cult of Osiris. Conflicts were often followed by brief periods of truce between the two parts of Egypt. This usually happened when a ruler from one of the dynasties died, as the throne had to pass to a new ruler.

The fifth king of the Eleventh Dynasty from Thebes—Mentuhotep II — swung the tide in favor of the south. He managed to subdue the nomarchs who ruled the contested lands that lay between the two capitals by exploiting an ongoing rebellion that had been launched against Memphis and took the city. One of the last kings of the Memphite Tenth Dynasty—Merikare or Merykare—died before Mentuhotep had reached the capital. Merikare's successor, whose name and even status remain unclear, lost the capital to the Theban ruler. Upon claiming the city, Mentuhotep II dismissed most of the local officials and was able to easily assert his control over the remainder of the northern territories, including the Nile Delta. Thus began a new era of ancient Egyptian history: the Middle Kingdom.

Chapter Three – The Middle Kingdom

The Middle Kingdom Period lasted from circa 2050 to 1650 BCE and was a period of Egyptian reunification after the turbulent era of the First Intermediate Period. Chronologically, this era typically includes the Eleventh and Twelfth Dynasties, which ruled from Thebes and Lisht (el-Lisht), respectively, though modern scholars also include the Thirteenth Dynasty well.

In any case, it is best to examine this period by looking at the individual reigns of the Egyptian kings during this time and point out the main characteristics that led to relative stability. Despite the abundance of evidence attesting to the rules of the Egyptian monarchs during the Middle Kingdom, a lot of compelling questions still remain.

Reunification under the Eleventh Dynasty

King Mentuhotep II from Thebes managed to defeat the rival nomarchs in both Upper and Lower Egypt and reunify the state once again in the 21st century BCE. This was a significant milestone that essentially saved the continuity of the Egyptian state, and it was recognized in ancient Egypt, with royal annals and inscriptions dating from the Twentieth Dynasty celebrating Mentuhotep II as a great ruler.

The abundance of relevant archaeological and written evidence from the reign of Mentuhotep II, also known as Nebhepetre, suggests that he was a successful king. His greatness is literally depicted in a relief in which the king towers over three other figures: his predecessor Intef III, his mother, and Kheti, a vizier who served during the reigns of Intef and Mentuhotep. The impressive figure of the king dwarfs the others, which points to his authority and importance, but it also might have been a deliberate effort to legitimize Mentuhotep II's rule as the successor of Intef III, as questions existed regarding his relationship to his predecessor.

These rumors were spread by the rival Lower Egypt kings from Heracleopolis. In fact, the existence of a violent conflict between Thebes and Heracleopolis is attested to by the discovery of a tomb of sixty soldiers close to the Mentuhotep's tomb. Additionally, we also know that Mentuhotep had to solidify his rule over more northern territories after his conquest of Memphis, as pockets of resistance were organized, possibly by King Merikare's successor. Thus, it seems logical that the northerners did not welcome their new king who was from a hostile rival house, prompting Mentuhotep to make an effort to strengthen his image as the legitimate king of the Two Lands.

There is also evidence that the king had to undertake military campaigns in Nubia and have a garrison ready on Elephantine, an island in the Nile, to eliminate all possible armed resistance efforts. Mentuhotep's other measures to boost his legitimacy can be observed in his name change, which most likely took place during his Sed festival. The king renamed himself Sematawy, which translates to "the unifier of two lands."

Mentuhotep II undertook significant administrative reforms that were aimed at boosting interconnectivity between the Egyptian lands, as well as strengthening the central authority of the pharaoh. Mentuhotep decided to rule from Thebes, which, compared to Memphis, was not large or prosperous. However, the king relied extensively on his viziers and allies when it came to control, introducing new offices for the governors of Lower and Upper Egypt. This measure was directed at reducing the influence of the nomarchs, who had been such a thorn in the side of the pharaohs. The king's vizier, Kheti, was one of the most active individuals in helping subdue unrest in the different nomes that arose with the accession of a new king. There is evidence of him leading Egyptian forces to the borders of the kingdom, perhaps in an effort to reestablish Egypt's authority in these areas, as well as contacting foreign societies to revive trade. This can explain the successful expedition to the Sinai Peninsula, which was a region of great interest and material importance for Egypt.

Mentuhotep ruled for an impressive fifty-one years. His rule was marked by the renewal of royal building projects that bore a resemblance to the greatness of the tombs and burial complexes of the kings of the Old Kingdom. Though pyramid-building was abandoned by this time, probably due to the costs associated with it, Mentuhotep built extensively throughout his reign. His mortuary complex at Deir el-Bahari remains the most interesting due to its scale and the innovative architectural elements that can be found throughout the complex.

Located west of Thebes, the mortuary complex of Mentuhotep was one of the first royal tombs to openly identify the king with Osiris. The innovative design of the complex features elements from both Theban and Memphite artists, whose works are differentiated by the clear distinctions in their style. For instance, the Theban style, which emphasizes large lips and eyes and uncharacteristically thin bodies, is apparent throughout the complex. Interestingly, however, the tombs reserved for the king's wives feature relief carvings characteristic of the Memphite style. The existence of such regional distinctions again points to the disunity of Egypt during the First Intermediate Period. Over time, the Memphite school would dominate other regional Egyptian styles.

Mentuhotep II was succeeded by his son, Mentuhotep III (c. 2004/9-1992/7 BCE), whose rule can also be characterized by the development of many different artistic forms and the undertaking of different ambitious building projects. His reign would essentially see the zenith of Middle Kingdom relief-carving techniques. However, the construction of his own tomb was never actually completed. Mentuhotep III constructed a mudbrick structure at a site called Thoth Hill on the west bank at Thebes, overlooking the Valley of Kings. The structure was probably commissioned in celebration of the Sed festival, though Mentuhotep III's reign was cut short before he could reach the milestone of ruling for thirty years. The structure might have been dedicated to the deity of Montu or Mentu, a hawk-headed god worshiped in Thebes. The name "Mentuhotep" translates to "Mentu is satisfied," so it is likely that the deity was worshiped by the rulers of the Eleventh Dynasty, who were themselves originally from Upper Egypt.

Other than his interest in building projects, the only undertaking that can be reliably attested to Mentuhotep III is the organization of an expedition to the Land of Punt, the territories southeast of Upper Egypt comprising the modern countries of Eritrea and Ethiopia. The expedition, led by commander Henenu, left behind an inscription at the site of Wadi

Hammamat. Punt was an important territory, as it was rich with resources like ivory and even gold. Old Kingdom kings had also sponsored campaigns to Punt to get a hold of the potential riches it could provide. Mentuhotep III's expedition reinvigorated Egyptian interest in Punt, leading to more expeditions.

Mentuhotep III was succeeded by Mentuhotep IV, who ascended the throne in the first decade of the 20th century BCE. He was likely an unrelated usurper and emerged as king after a succession struggle. Not much is known about his reign. If the Turin Canon is to be believed, he only became king about seven years after the death of his predecessor. Nevertheless, Mentuhotep IV organized further expeditions into Punt, one of which was led by a man named Amenemhat, who managed to establish wells with fresh water in the desert regions east of Upper Egypt. Amenemhat, a vizier or a person with high status, appears to have succeeded the throne as the first king of the Twelfth Dynasty, further stressing the instability that might have been associated with Mentuhotep IV's reign.

The Twelfth Dynasty

The details behind Amenemhat's emergence as the next king of Egypt remain unclear. He assumed the throne sometime during the first decade of the 20th century BCE, but we can't say for sure whether or not he was involved in a direct military confrontation with Mentuhotep IV. The "evidence" we have of this period is the *Prophecy of Neferti*, a literary text that was composed around the same time as the establishment of the Twelfth Dynasty. The text supposedly points out the major problems in Egypt and predicts that a figure named Ameny will emerge from the south and end the crisis. It mentions that Ameny will take both the red and the white crowns, thus unifying Upper and Lower Egypt. It also claims that the new ruler will face enemies from Libya and Asia but that he will protect his lands by the construction of defensive "walls of the ruler" against the invaders.

It is not difficult to guess that the supposed savior and unifier of Egypt, Ameny, is identified with King Amenemhat. Coming from a non-royal background, it is probable that the king needed to legitimize his accession to the throne. The "prophecy" might have been composed after Amenemhat had already established his control over Egypt, so it is not exactly strange that everything mentioned in the text resembles the truth.

One of the first and most important decisions made by King Amenemhat was the relocation of the state's capital from Thebes farther to the north to the new town of Amenemhat-itj-tawy or just Itjtawy. We don't know for sure where Itjtawy was exactly located. The most probable explanation suggests that the pharaoh's new residence was near the Lisht necropolis in the Faiyum region, close to the Nile Delta. Lisht would become an important site for royal burials during the Twelfth Dynasty, as it contained the pyramid complexes of both Amenemhat and his successor, Senusret I. The strategic importance of the new capital has to be stressed. It was closer to the center of the realm and on the crossroads from the heart of Egypt toward Asia. It also marked a clear political break from the Eleventh Dynasty, which was concentrated around Thebes, and acted as a statement from the new king about the beginning of a new era—a theme that was prominent during his reign.

Amenemhat was seen as the restorer of order and the former glory of the realm. For instance, his Horus name, Wehemmesu, means "rebirth" or "renaissance." Amenemhat wanted to establish a connection to the glory days of the Egyptian civilization, the Age of Pyramids during the Old Kingdom, when the pharaohs' might and authority were at their highest. The Twelfth Dynasty rulers, beginning with Amenemhat, would be increasingly influenced by the Old Kingdom period, alluding to its greatness in literary sources, trying to emphasize the supreme divine nature of the pharaoh, and borrowing its architectural and artistic styles. Invocation of such imagery and allusions creates a feeling that Mentuhotep IV's reign was perceived to be largely unsuccessful and maybe even illegitimate and that Amenemhat, his former vizier, had manipulated the dubious political conditions in his favor to become king.

King Amenemhat I constructed several defensive structures throughout the kingdom, perhaps in an effort to further consolidate his rule. It is probable that the "walls of the ruler" mentioned in the *Prophecy of Neferti* existed; they might have been located somewhere in the northeastern part of Lower Egypt. Though no archaeological evidence of a defensive structure from this time has been discovered there, it would have made sense to have a fortification established on the border to keep watch on prospective invaders from Asia. Amenemhat also launched campaigns to the south into the Nubian territories later in his reign. The chief motivation behind these military expeditions was the assertion of Egyptian dominance over the neighboring lands that were rich in raw materials, especially gold.

Amenemhat I was succeeded by his son, Senusret I. Manetho mentions that the king died as a result of a conspiracy that succeeded in assassinating him. The existence of a conspiracy and the assassination of Amenemhat I is also attested to in the famous "Teachings of Amenemhat" ("Instructions of Amenemhat"), a poem composed at around the same time as Amenemhat's death. The poem features the ghost of the already deceased Amenemhat I appearing in front of Senusret I, telling the new king the story of his murder and instructing him to always be on alert.

It is not unlikely that the poem was written on the orders of Senusret, not only as a source of legitimization but also as a means to "expose" the conspirators complicit in the murder of his father. This would have been important for Senusret, as he was on a military campaign to Libya when he learned of his father's death. Amenemhat had made him a co-ruler sometime before his death. The conspirators could have killed Amenemhat to exclude Senusret from the succession. Senusret would have justified his elimination of his supposed enemies through the poem, which features Amenemhat talking about the conspiracy:

"It was after supper, when night had fallen, and I had spent an hour of happiness. I was asleep upon my bed, having become weary, and my heart had begun to follow sleep. When weapons of my counsel were wielded, I had become like a snake of the necropolis. As I came to, I awoke to fighting, and I found that it was an attack of the bodyguard. If I had quickly taken weapons in my hand, I would have made the wretches retreat with a charge! But there is none mighty in the night, none who can fight alone; no success will come without a helper. Look, my injury happened while I was without you, when the entourage had not yet heard that I would hand over to you when I had not yet sat with you, that I might make counsels for you; for I did not plan it; I did not foresee it, and my heart had not taken thought of the negligence of servants."

In the spirit of the Old Kingdom rulers, Senusret I undertook an array of building projects, constructing temples and shrines all over the kingdom. The need to finance these projects and provide sufficient building materials for them might have been the reason behind the extensive military campaigns under his reign. Senusret's expeditions reached Sinai, lower Nubia, and Kush, collecting valuables such as gold, ivory, copper, and turquoise. This booty was then transferred to the various ongoing building sites. During Senusret's reign, the royal style of relief carving and architecture again become prominent throughout Egypt, eclipsing local styles. Construction also began on the Karnak Temple

Complex, located at Thebes, which would be expanded upon by later rulers and would emerge as a distinct spiritual center of Egypt. Senusret erected the White Chapel at Karnak, a small temple with fine relief carvings that was constructed to commemorate the Sed festival of the king, who reigned for over forty years.

The Height of the Middle Kingdom

Senusret I was followed by Amenemhat II (c. 1929–1895 BCE), the events of whose reign are known to us thanks to the discovery of royal annals at Memphis. The annals stress the relationship between Egypt and the neighboring regions. It can be assumed that Egyptian influence reached well into western Asia during this period. Several cities of the Levant and Mesopotamia established trade relations with Egypt, something that has been confirmed by the abundance of Egyptian relics in the Sinai and the Palestine region. Several Egyptian statuettes and scarabs have been discovered in these areas, making it clear that links between Egypt and cities like Byblos existed during Amenemhat II's reign.

Inscriptions in the king's royal tomb also mention the organization of military campaigns, especially in the south. These expeditions reached the kingdoms of Kush and Punt, probably with the aim of reimposing Egyptian influence on these territories. Other than that, not much is known about the nature of Amenemhat II's rule. One peculiarity is the lack of royal building projects, especially when considering the extensive construction projects undertaken by his predecessors. The White Pyramid at Dahshur is one of the only examples, though the pyramid is largely in ruins. Its materials were extracted for other uses by robbers throughout the centuries.

Amenemhat made his son, Senusret II, his co-ruler. He died two years later. Senusret II ruled for about two decades, and his reign was also characterized by peace and stability. Senusret II began working on one of the most ambitious projects at Faiyum, developing a complex irrigation system that greatly boosted agricultural production in the region. The project included digging canals that connected the Faiyum Oasis, located west of the Nile, with the waters of Lake Moeris. This resulted in reclaiming a huge piece of land that became arable. Investment in domestic projects such as this improved the Egyptian economy and paved the way for further strengthening the Egyptian state under his successor, Senusret III.

The Middle Kingdom reached the zenith of its power during the reign of Senusret III, who, according to the Turin King List, reigned for over thirty years, from around 1870 to 1831 BCE. Senusret III was a warrior king and participated in several military campaigns, mostly against Nubia, during his sixth, eighth, tenth, and sixteenth regnal years. The king set up victory stelae in Nubian territories in the south at the fortified sites of Semna and Uronarti. The purpose of these stelae was to remind the locals of Senusret III's authority and his bloody military ventures, which supposedly resulted in the total domination of the Nubians. In order to maintain his interests in the region, Senusret built several defensive structures that were garrisoned to keep watch of travelers who entered the Egyptian territories from the south. The network of forts eventually developed its own identity and became increasingly interconnected with each other. Some, like Mirgissa, served as Egyptian trading outposts, where locals exchanged various goods, while others only kept their military roles and were used as supply checkpoints along the southern border.

In addition to Nubia, Senusret's military activities were directed against the Aamu, the Egyptian term used to describe the western Asian people as a whole. Earlier campaigns into the Levant had resulted in an increasing number of prisoners from the lands of Canaan, something that is attested to in a tomb painting of a royal official by the name of Khnumhotep. Khnumhotep's tomb at Beni Hasan, which dates back to the early Twelfth Dynasty, shows the procession of a group of the Aamu, who were either brought as war prisoners or were nomadic peoples who had settled in Egypt. Nevertheless, during the Middle Kingdom, Egyptian kings campaigned extensively against the Aamu despite having extensive trade links with them.

Senusret III is often credited with strengthening the institution of the king at the expense of weakening the nomarchs. Though this is largely true, as Egypt certainly became more centralized during the monarch's reign, the decline of the nomes had been in the making for a long time. Since the end of the First Intermediate Period, several different kings had tried to reduce the influence of the nomarchs, who were essentially scapegoated for the destruction of the unified state created by the Old Kingdom. In the eyes of the Middle Kingdom rulers, the Old Kingdom was romanticized, so it is natural that the nomarchs, who held considerable sway and power, were actively challenged by the kings during this time.

As early as Mentuhotep II's reign, disfavored nomarchs were removed from positions of power. At that time, the regional identities and rivalries between different parts of Egypt were still very pronounced, and considering the strong influence of Thebes during the Eleventh Dynasty, it is logical that nomarchs unsympathetic to the Theban rulers were treated poorly. Over time, the Egyptian kings began to reshuffle the administrative system in a way that resulted in the decline of the nomarchs' power. During the reign of Amenemhat I, the nomarchs were centrally appointed, though their competency as regional overlords was limited because of the increase in the influence of major towns as administrative centers. A new office of the mayor was created, which was responsible for governing these urban centers. This was seen as a direct hit to the power of the nomarchs, who relied on their extensive land ownership to accrue wealth. During the reign of Senusret II, the king began to take the nomarchs' sons to educate them in the capital under his supervision.

By the time of Senusret III, only a couple of nomarchs retained their positions in the state hierarchy. The king proceeded to create new institutions to further take power away from the nomarchs. These institutions, which oversaw the collection of taxes or the organization of armies and labor forces, were run by state-appointed bureaucrats. As long as the growth of the state bureaucracy was kept in check, Senusret and his successors could avoid the concentration of power in the hands of individuals and control corruption.

The reign of Senusret III marks the height of the political power of the Middle Kingdom, thanks to the successful military campaigns of the king in neighboring areas and the end of the nomarchs. This state of affairs spilled over into the reign of Amenemhat III, who ascended the throne in the middle of the 19th century BCE. Amenemhat III had shared the throne with his father for about twenty years, which allowed him to be involved in many of the major decisions taken by Senusret III. Since Egypt was enjoying a period of prosperity, Amenemhat directed his efforts to more building projects, including the further development of the irrigation systems at Faiyum. He built two pyramid complexes at Dahshur and Hawara, in addition to his colossal statues at the Faiyum Oasis, which were described by Herodotus but have been destroyed.

Amenemhat III's reign is marked by an abundance of culturally significant artifacts, including several well-preserved statues of the pharaoh that feature interesting and unique designs. The king also extensively sponsored the undertaking of mining activities throughout Egyptian lands and in the regions of the Sinai Peninsula, Punt, Nubia, and Kush. Quarry sites such as Wadi Hammamat, Aswan, and others became centers of Egyptian industry, producing valuable materials such as copper, turquoise, limestone, alabaster, and amethyst.

Culture and Society during the Middle Kingdom

Before we examine the causes behind the decline of the Middle Kingdom, it is important to emphasize the many different cultural and socioeconomic developments that shaped the Middle Kingdom. We have already broadly touched upon these subjects, such as the establishment of close trading contacts with the neighboring regions of the Levant, Punt, and Nubia, as well as the development of the Egyptian bureaucracy that further centralized power in the hands of the king. Upon taking a closer look, however, we can see many important cultural changes, something that can be observed in the prominence of new deities and the development of different artistic forms.

Middle Kingdom rulers were patrons of the cult of Osiris. Osiris became a chief deity. He was involved with the affairs of the afterlife and was elevated to the protector of royal necropolises and religious centers. The pharaohs were considered to have united with Osiris after their death.

Cultural centers, such as Abydos, were granted immense importance during the Middle Kingdom. Abydos peaked during the reign of Senusret III, who constructed a royal tomb there. This mortuary complex is rather extensive and is located on top of a hill and surrounded by the residences of religious and state officials. Abydos was one of the original places in Egypt that had a cult of Osiris. In later centuries, Abydos gained more prominence as an important religious and even a political center.

The promotion of the cult of Osiris was also associated with many developments in funerary practices. There is evidence in Abydos of ordinary people taking part in funerary rites and rituals that had previously been only reserved for pharaohs. A new importance was placed on the afterlife as a whole, and there was an increased number of Coffin Texts. These texts are similar to the inscriptions found in royal tombs and on pyramid walls that talk about the deceased's deeds. More importantly, the prominence of the cult of Osiris resulted in the belief that all people had *ba*, the unique aspect of the individual's soul that would live on after death. This is attested in what is arguably the earliest literary text exploring the topic of suicide, which dates back to the Middle Kingdom, "The Dispute between a Man and His Ba." The text is typical of the powerful, deeply philosophical literature characteristic of the Middle Kingdom. In it, the main character talks about the problems he is facing in his life, expressing his desire to die and tackle the benefits of the unknown that is death while speaking to his soul, or *ba*.

The existence of such texts and the so-called "democratization of beliefs" suggests the development of personal piety. This stresses personal relationships with gods instead of going through the mediation of other figures, such as priests or the king, who claimed to represent the divinity of the deities. The notion of deep personal beliefs and their expressions would become even more important during the New Kingdom, as ancient Egypt would experience its first crisis of faith.

Interestingly, the development of such a concept is similar to what transpired in Christianity with the Protestant Reformation more than 2,500 years later. Protestant reformers emphasized the necessity for all believers to establish personal connections with God through their own beliefs, reducing their reliance on religious officials who no longer had to act as mediators between the believers and God.

The promotion of the cult of Osiris was also reflected in the advancement of the designs of the mortuary complexes and royal tombs. We have to remember that decisions regarding the architectural styles of the tombs reflected their religious beliefs, prompting further developments in techniques and craftsmanship. There is considerable evidence of experimentation of different designs that pushed the limits of ancient Egyptian techniques and resulted in the construction of memorable temple complexes with unique styles. These can be observed in the terraced design of Mentuhotep II's temple at Deir el-Bahari, located at the Theban necropolis. This was not only the case for royal tombs; burial complexes of nomarchs from the Eleventh Dynasty also feature unique designs, including artworks that depict the nomarchs' lives. Their coffins are often elevated from the ground, where their subordinates and members of their court are buried. On the whole, however, there was an increase in the number of special tombs for non-privileged individuals, leading to an increase in the size of regional necropolises.

Advancements in religious thought and practices went hand in hand with other cultural achievements, most importantly in writing. The tradition of ancient Egyptian literature essentially originated in the Middle Kingdom, and many compelling texts were composed during the Eleventh and Twelfth Dynasties. Religious and philosophical texts were the most popular.

More importantly, thanks to the expansion of Egypt's bureaucracy and the emergence of more people into what can roughly be called a "middle class," there was an increase in the number of everyday texts. These included everything from letters, accounts, and reports to administrative decrees. These works provide us with information about the everyday lives of ancient Egyptians. It also suggests a rise in the literacy level, which helped Egypt become a cultural powerhouse later on.

Thanks to newer and firmer contacts with other societies of the ancient world, including with western Asia and the Aegean communities, the Egyptians were exposed to a wide range of different cultures and ideas. As a result, Egyptian society became more dynamic, something that was accelerated by the reforms of the pharaohs and the transformation of central belief systems. This balance is what makes the Middle Kingdom so compelling to examine. It was an era of rebuilding and reuniting ancient Egypt. Old Kingdom ideas and concepts greatly influenced the decisions of the most prominent leaders of Egypt during this period.

However, far more destabilizing times were to come as the Twelfth Dynasty came to an end.

The Fall of the Middle Kingdom

The Middle Kingdom reached its political, cultural, and socioeconomic peak during the reigns of Senusret III and Amenemhat III. After that, it began its slow and painful decline into what is now known as the Second Intermediate Period. The cyclical nature of ancient Egyptian history, where an era of prosperity and stability was disrupted by periods of crisis, is a good interpretation of the historical events of the era, and it was perceived as thus by ancient Egyptians themselves.

The confusion and chaos that is associated with such transitions is present at the end of the Middle Kingdom. There are still many questions regarding the nature and duration of kings after Amenemhat III. What complicates things even more is the fact that unlike when the Old Kingdom declined, the fall of the Middle Kingdom was also caused by external factors. This leads to distorted and contested perspectives. Broader elements of ancient Egypt during this time can be attested to but not in a lot of detail.

Amenemhat III was succeeded by Amenemhat IV at a time when Egyptian statehood was still relatively secure. The short reign of the king might be due to the fact that he ascended the throne at an old age. The lack of any significant developments undertaken by Amenemhat IV is not surprising. He evidently left no male heirs and was succeeded by his sister (and possibly his wife), Sobekneferu or Neferusobek, who became the first historically attested female pharaoh of ancient Egypt. She ruled for just over three years. Her name means "beauty of Sobek," a deity with a crocodile head in ancient Egyptian mythology. Sobek was associated with fertility and the Nile River. Sobek was a prominent deity in the Faiyum region, as he was believed to protect the people from the overflowing Nile. The use of Sobek's name by Queen Sobekneferu further proves the importance of Faiyum during the Middle Kingdom, and it also might hint at problems caused by the Nile around the same time.

Whatever the case, complexities began to arise with the death of Sobekneferu, who left no heirs and was replaced by Sobekhotep I, who is considered to be the founder of the Thirteenth Dynasty. The political situation that appears to have emerged in Egypt at the time of this transition greatly resembles the situation after the death of Pepi II. There was a succession of several pharaohs whose reigns were short-lived and unstable. The lack of an actual heir related by blood to the queen or her predecessors was most likely the main cause of these problems.

Interestingly, the kings of the Thirteenth Dynasty were not related to each other by blood. Some of them came from the state bureaucracy and the court of previous pharaohs. They ruled the state for a brief period of time. That is why we don't know much about the nature of the reigns other than the names of the kings themselves. The deity Sobek features in their names too, suggesting a conscious effort by these rulers to legitimize their position by using the same name as Queen Sobekneferu. What can also be observed during this period is the gradual collapse of a centralized state, meaning that the kings, from wherever they ruled, did not exercise effective control over the entirety of Egypt.

Throughout much of the 18th century BCE, the southern boundary of Egypt continued to be pulled back more northward, suggesting that the kings did not have the power and resources to maintain effective rule over the southernmost areas. Neferhotep I, who ruled for a period of eleven years sometime during the second half of the 18th century, is one of the best-attested rulers of this time. He was able to maintain somewhat firm control over the territories of Lower Egypt and most likely reasserted Egyptian influence in the Levant, something that can be shown by the existence of a stela of the governor of Byblos, Yantin. Some scholars believe that Byblos was still in the Egyptian sphere of influence during this time, though this notion is often challenged.

Sometime during the Thirteenth Dynasty, the already declining Egyptian authority began to be challenged by outsiders. Despite Amenemhat I's efforts to contain the threat of incursions through the construction of defensive structures on the eastern Nile Delta, more foreigners began to enter Egypt. These peoples were nomadic Semitic tribes who settled in the eastern delta, where they assimilated with Egyptian culture and were mostly present in and around the site of Avaris, the later seat of the foreign Hyksos kings.

Part of the reason behind their migration into Egypt was the increasing enslavement of Asian people during the military campaigns of the Middle Kingdom. This resulted in many Egyptian families possessing tens of Asian slaves, who, over time, became members of Egyptian society.

Freed slaves probably achieved recognition by getting involved in warfare, where they emerged as military leaders, leading to their eventual accession to the throne of Egypt. One of the earliest such Semitic rulers (possibly the first one) went by the name of Khendjer. He ruled for a short period of about five years but constructed a pyramid at Saqqara. This points to the power center of the Thirteenth Dynasty being near Memphis or even at el-Lisht, though it is impossible to arrive at a cohesive narrative of the situation at the time. Considering such factors, it is not difficult to see why certain scholars believe the end of the Twelfth Dynasty to be the "unofficial" beginning of the Second Intermediate Period.

The beginning of the 17th century BCE saw even more important developments in ancient Egypt. Indo-Aryan migrations in western Asia triggered a series of displacements of different peoples in the Near East, something that also affected the social makeup of Egypt. Such displacements led to the arrival of the western Semitic Hyksos into Egyptian territories.

The name Hyksos was first used by Manetho, and it was most likely an adaptation of the word *hekau khasut*, which means "rulers of foreign lands." The Hyksos migrated to Egypt from the Levant. Many scholars have identified them as Canaanite peoples, ancestors of the Jews. Whatever the case, they arrived in Egypt in increasing numbers throughout the 17th century, settling at Avaris and emerging as dominant actors in Egyptian politics.

The success of the Hyksos was in large part caused by their access to better military technology, which allowed them to dominate their rivals. However, they did not necessarily wage wars against the Thirteenth

Dynasty rulers of the Second Intermediate Period upon their arrival. Their settlement in Avaris was natural, given the international and, more specifically, Asian makeup of the city. Avaris quickly grew to become one of the largest cities in northern Egypt.

If we consider the uncertain political situation present in Egypt at the time of the takeover of Avaris, it is possible that the group of people identified as the Hyksos were a smaller group of elites who defeated the Egyptian rulers of Avaris, who are referred to as the Fourteenth Dynasty.

However, the extent of the Hyksos rule was limited. They most likely only ruled the eastern delta region, where a lot of Semitic settlements began to be founded during the 17th and 16th centuries BCE. Despite this, the Hyksos claimed sovereignty over all of Egypt, exploiting the fragmented nature of the state at the time. It is likely that they managed to establish their rule over other parts of Egypt through puppet or vassal dynasties, such as the Sixteenth Dynasty based in Thebes.

The Turin King List mentions that there were only six Hyksos rulers who ruled directly from Avaris for a period of about 150 years. Khyan or Khian's reign is best attested. Interestingly, there are objects bearing his name that have been discovered in a wide range of locations, including at Gebelein, south of Thebes, which suggests either Khyan's suzerainty over Upper Egypt or some form of trade relations between Avaris and Thebes. Additionally, Hyksos artifacts from this period extend to Knossos at Crete, Baghdad, and Hattusa, the latter of which was the capital of the Anatolian Hittite Empire. Royal Hyksos scarabs have also been discovered in large numbers in the Levant, suggesting that ties between this area and Egypt never ceased during this time.

Like many of the other conquerors of Egypt, the Hyksos largely appropriated the Egyptian culture and way of life, introducing minor changes in the administration. They took the full pharaonic titles and worshiped the deity Seth, much like other western Semitic inhabitants of Avaris and the eastern Nile Delta. The Hyksos introduced a range of military tactics and technologies that became a staple of Egyptian warfare in later centuries. For instance, they introduced the composite bow design and battle chariots drawn by horses, which made the armies more mobile. Additionally, the closer ties to the Levant and the Near East regions resulted in an increasing exchange of ideas, customs, and practices, which would greatly influence Egypt after the end of the Second Intermediate Period.

Chapter Four – The New Kingdom

In this chapter, we will take a look at the almost five-century-long period of ancient Egypt known as the New Kingdom or the Egyptian Empire. This era of ancient Egyptian history bears a lot of resemblance to the preceding Middle and Old Kingdom periods, boasting a rich material and cultural heritage. The New Kingdom is noted for some of the most well-known pharaohs, such as Akhenaten and his wife Nefertiti, Tutankhamun, and Ramesses II.

Defeating the Hyksos

The Second Intermediate Period lasted roughly to the mid-16th century BCE. The Hyksos dynasty, with its seat at Avaris, dominated Egypt during this time, though it focused most of its activities in the northern part of the state, mostly around the Nile Delta region. Hyksos rulers were considered to be foreigners by Egyptians, especially in Upper Egypt, where their influence was not as prevalent. Upper Egyptian lands were ruled by puppet rulers based in Thebes, and they did not necessarily get along with Avaris, though there was little resistance from their side during the late 17th century BCE. While looking at evidence from this period, many scholars have suggested that the Theban rulers acted independently from the Hyksos, something that is possible if we consider the developments during the middle of the 16th century. About thirty years into the reign of Hyksos King Apophis or Apepi, who ascended the throne around 1575 BCE, Theban scribes called their local rulers "king" while the Hyksos continued to refer to them as "prince." This stems from the fact that the Theban ruling family assumed the royal titles and established their own dynasty (the Sixteenth Dynasty) in Thebes to counterbalance the foreign rule in Avaris.

Little other than names of the rulers are known from the Sixteenth Dynasty, which lasted until around 1580 BCE when the Hyksos supposedly asserted their rule over them. It was succeeded by the Seventeenth Dynasty, established also around 1580 BCE, which was also centered around Thebes and in direct opposition with the Hyksos. Most rulers of Thebes from this time were relatively undistinguished, though their sphere of influence appears to have included Abydos farther to the north. The last two kings of the Seventeenth Dynasty began to fight for their independence against their Hyksos suzerains.

Around 1550 BCE, King Seqenenre Tao was the first to engage in military skirmishes with the northern overlords. In fact, the wounded face of his mummy, now residing in the Egyptian Museum in Cairo, suggests that he was a victim of one of the engagements. Seqenenre Tao was succeeded by his son, Kamose, who continued to wage war against the Hyksos. He had some relative success. The campaign is recounted in great detail on the two stelae erected by the king at Abydos, as well as on the Carnarvon Tablet, which was discovered in 1908. According to these inscriptions, King Kamose defied his royal counsel and decided to wage war against the Hyksos, refusing to be intimidated by the northern rulers. Kamose expresses his desire for revenge, as he cannot tolerate being a simple "prince" who has to share Egyptian land with foreigners. The details of the campaigns are also included. Kamose led a flotilla of ships down the Nile and managed to conquer the city of Nefrusy before pushing to Avaris farther to the north. Though the Hyksos were able to defend Avaris and force the king back, their position was significantly damaged by this campaign. Supposedly, they sent a messenger to the Kingdom of Kush, south of the Upper Egypt territories, to request aid against the Theban king, but the messenger never managed to relay the call for help, as he was captured.

After the death of Kamose around 1539 BCE, he was succeeded by his brother, Ahmose I, who ascended the throne under favorable circumstances. His succession coincided with the death of Hyksos King Apophis, who had ruled for a very long time. The Hyksos were also likely weakened after attacks by the Hittite Empire on their distant dependencies in the Levant. Ahmose quickly renewed the war effort against the Hyksos. The reconquest of the north was completed after the fall of both Memphis and Avaris.

Ahmose also took control of the delta region before assembling a force comprised of war chariots and taking the fight to the Levant. The aim of this campaign was most likely to secure the copper mines located in Syria, as well as to probably dissuade any idea of further attacks by the Canaanites. Thus, the Hyksos were defeated and expelled from Egypt, and the two parts of the state were reunified once again by King Ahmose I. He became the founder of the Nineteenth Dynasty and ushered in the era of the New Kingdom.

The defeat of the Hyksos was not Ahmose's only achievement during his reign, which lasted until around 1525 BCE. He also campaigned in Lower Nubia, something that is attested by the inscriptions from Kush bearing his name. Ahmose, like most of his predecessors, wanted Egypt to control this land because of its rich quarries and gold mines, which were essential for the economic strength of Egypt. The king installed a subordinate ruler to watch over the territory, making it essentially dependent on Egypt for the next few centuries. He also sponsored the development of Middle Kingdom fortifications on the southern border, which had been left unmaintained during the Second Intermediate Period.

Having asserted his control over all of Egypt and the neighboring regions of interest, Ahmose implemented several reforms in order to bring the administration back up to the standard of the Twelfth Dynasty bureaucracy. His efforts ultimately resulted in many of the most important offices becoming hereditary. The king also paid great attention to the development of Thebes and Abydos as the political and cultural centers of Egypt, a process that was greatly accelerated by his successor, Amenhotep I (c. 1514–1493 BCE).

Amenhotep I's reign saw the revival of Egyptian culture and arts. Many art forms and statues produced during this time bear great resemblance to the styles of the early Middle Kingdom. His court was full of a wide range of writers, poets, physicians, architects, and scientists who were lucky enough to enjoy the patronage of the king. This led to the production of the Ebers Papyrus, which was important in reconstructing the chronology of the New Kingdom and also contains extensive information about the medical practices of ancient Egypt. His architect, Ineni, oversaw the construction and expansion of the Karnak Temple Complex. He also began work on the Valley of Kings, a rock-cut necropolis where most of the royal tombs of the New Kingdom are located.

An important literary text composed during Amenhotep I's reign is the *Amduat*, "The Book of the Underworld," which tells the story of the sun god Ra's daily journey through the underworld, from the time the sun sets to the time it rises again. The *Amduat* describes the different sections of the underworld in great detail, stressing the regions reserved for those condemned to eternal torture and damnation. The text became of paramount importance to the Egyptian culture, and its parts were subsequently reproduced in most of the royal tombs of the New Kingdom. This was due to the rising popularity of the cult of Ra, which was beginning to be identified with the pharaoh, and the belief that Osiris was a nocturnal reincarnation of Ra in the underworld.

Amenhotep I was succeeded by Thutmose I, who ascended the throne in the late 16th or early 15th century BCE. He ruled for about twelve years. He is most remembered for his aggressive foreign policy, which resulted in a series of military campaigns against Egypt's enemies. Thutmose's armies launched offensives in the Levant, challenging the newly emergent Mitanni Kingdom in Mesopotamia and reaching, for the first time in Egyptian history, the Euphrates River. The pharaoh also led his forces to the south, crossing the traditional border point and reaching the Fourth Cataract of the Nile, which is now located in the territory of Sudan. This campaign resulted in the subjugation of Lower Nubia or Kush. The vizier Turi became a local ruler; he had total control over these lands, like a viceroy. These successful endeavors greatly enriched the royal treasury and contributed to the extension of Egypt's sphere of influence.

Domestically, Thutmose I's reign was marked by more building projects at Karnak, including the construction of several obelisks and colonnades that significantly altered the design of the temple. The chief architect of Thutmose's court, Ineni, was involved in the construction of these and other projects, such as the temples at Abydos and Memphis. Interestingly, Memphis became a sort of military headquarters. The capital was still at Thebes.

The architect Ineni also oversaw the construction of the king's tomb at the Valley of Kings. Thutmose I was most likely the first ruler who was buried in the necropolis. While the remains of his original mortuary temple did not survive, there is evidence of his tomb after the pharaoh's reburial by Thutmose III about forty years after Thutmose was buried.

The Might of the Eighteenth Dynasty

Ahmose I, Amenhotep I, and Thutmose I laid the foundations for a politically dominant and militarily aggressive Egyptian state, catapulting ancient Egypt to the height of its power. Thutmose I's son, Thutmose II, would ascend the throne sometime in the first decade of the 15th century BCE, ruling for a period of about thirteen years. Just like his predecessors, Thutmose II campaigned in Palestine and Nubia, reasserting Egyptian power in these regions. He also contributed to the development of the Karnak Temple Complex.

The pharaoh died without a son from his chief royal wife, Queen Hatshepsut, circa 1479, resulting in the throne passing to a son from his lesser wife, Thutmose III, who was just two years old when he inherited the kingdom. Interestingly, Hatshepsut served as regent for the boy before he came of age. She co-ruled with Thutmose III for about two decades.

Queen Hatshepsut, who would bear the full royal title just a couple of years into her regency, would officially be proclaimed as pharaoh, a traditionally masculine role. Queen Sobekneferu had ruled Egypt for some time during the Twelfth Dynasty, but the grandeur and might of Hatshepsut's reign had never been seen before under a female ruler.

The kingship (or queenship) of Hatshepsut marked a turning point in the notion of Egyptian kingship as a whole. During the Old and Middle Kingdoms, the role of the pharaoh was well defined. Hatshepsut still had to conform to the traditional Egyptian understanding of what it meant to be a pharaoh. For instance, in her depictions, she possesses all of the male pharaonic symbols and regalia, such as the pharaonic head cloth and a false beard. This served to boost her legitimacy. Moreover, the walls of her mortuary temple contain markings that assert it was not her own decision to assume the position of the pharaoh; it had been the intention of her father, Thutmose I. Yet, despite such decisions, Hatshepsut expressed her femininity whenever she could. For example, she adopted the name the "daughter of Ra" among her royal titles.

For the next twenty years after her proclamation as pharaoh, Hatshepsut succeeded in essentially usurping the royal power for herself. The young Thutmose III held no actual influence despite being a nominal co-ruler with his aunt and stepmother. To be fair, the blatant promotion of her as the rightful pharaoh went hand in hand with the constant reassertion by Hatshepsut that Thutmose III was the legitimate successor of the throne.

Thanks to the help of some of her closest allies and ministers, such as the High Priest of Amun Hapuseneb, her hold over the domestic and foreign policies of Egypt never wavered. It also helped that she was a rather successful ruler who did not rely on military conquests like her predecessors. Instead, Hatshepsut's efforts were directed toward increasing trade relations with neighboring regions. This is attested to by one of her expeditions to the Land of Punt around 1471 BCE, which resulted in the reestablishment of trade routes and the import of valuable materials such as ebony, gold, and incense. Domestically, one of the major changes during her reign was the rejection of the cult of the god Seth, who had become an important deity during the rule of the Hyksos. She promoted the cult of Amun, the deity that was later fused with the sun god Ra. Representing herself as the daughter of Amun-Ra, she expanded the temple of the deity at Karnak and erected two granite obelisks at the site.

Historians have debated whether the end of Hatshepsut's reign was caused by a coup d'état organized by Thutmose III and his allies or whether the transition of power was peaceful and caused by the eventual death of the queen around 1458 BCE. Hatshepsut is known to have ruled largely thanks to the extensive network of relations she had forged with some of her chief ministers, including her architect Senenmut, whose tomb features an interesting and lavish design pointing to his role. Her other confidants, such as her vizier Useramun, appear to have maintained their roles after Thutmose III came of age.

Much later, Hatshepsut's reign would be viewed by ancient Egyptians as shameful and illegitimate, leading to the destruction of many of her monuments and even to the omission of the queen from the king lists. Nevertheless, Hatshepsut's reign was one of the most unique. The queen, while not undertaking many military campaigns, was able to keep the realm together during times of uncertainty, something that resulted in a compelling legacy.

One of the greatest warriors and military leaders in all of ancient Egyptian history, King Thutmose III, began his sole reign sometime between 1458 and 1457 BCE. Thutmose III recognized that being passive in foreign matters for the past two decades had resulted in the weakening of the pharaoh's authority over the Egyptian territories in western Asia. The Mitanni, with the help of local cities, threatened Egyptian positions in the Levant, prompting the king to undertake a campaign to the city of Megiddo just months into his sole rule. After a ruthless seven-month-long siege of the city and after the total casualty toll exceeded over ten thousand people (this is a modern estimate), Thutmose III was victorious. The Egyptian army took valuable loot from the city, including hundreds of war chariots that could be used for further campaigns.

This would be the first of Thutmose's military endeavors. By the end of his reign, he is believed to have ventured on seventeen expeditions in total. The details of what transpired during these campaigns were inscribed on temple walls, obelisks, and stelae constructed by the pharaoh, who, much like his predecessors, built extensively in Karnak.

The statue of Thutmose III at the Luxor Museum.'

In his later campaigns, the king was able to consolidate his control over the territories in Syria, imposing tribute on some of the most important city-states of the region, places where Egypt wrestled for influence with the Hittites and Mitanni. By establishing a network of garrisons, Thutmose III could transport his forces by sea to Byblos in modern-day Lebanon, from where he launched further campaigns to quell any rebellions that popped up in the contested areas. Cities like Aleppo, Kadesh, and Carchemish significantly weakened the power of the Mitanni, who were unable to defend their territories from the Egyptian armies. In the conquered territories, a tighter system of royal control was imposed, though the ruling princes of the cities mostly kept their sovereignty in exchange for paying tribute. Family members of Asian princes were taken to the Egyptian court and harem so the king could have decent leverage over his Canaanite vassals, who were prone to rebel. Thutmose III's military endeavors concluded with a campaign in the south during the second half of his reign. Campaigning in Nubia and reaching the Fourth Cataract of the Nile, Thutmose made sure that the flow of Nubian gold into his treasury was steady and undisrupted.

Thutmose III was responsible for greatly extending the borders of his realm. During his reign, Egypt completed its transformation into the well-oiled militaristic society that would come to dominate its rivals for the next few centuries. This direction was a conscious decision by Thutmose III, who made sure that his son and eventual successor, Amenhotep II, acknowledged the importance of his father's deeds. The pharaoh spent a lot of time with his son, notably in Memphis rather than Thebes due to the city's proximity to the front lines and the militaristic role the city had assumed. Egypt developed a new identity in which the role of the military elites was more pronounced than ever before.

King Thutmose III's extensive campaigns did not mean that he neglected his other pharaonic duties. He expanded the Temple of Amun at Karnak, and the deity continued to play a central role in the Egyptian belief system. His temples, stelae, and obelisks bear markings that talk about the glorious campaigns of the king. They also stress the importance of the deity Montu, the embodiment of the pharaoh's strength and a warrior god.

The influence of his education and upbringing manifested very clearly when Amenhotep II ascended the throne between 1427 and 1426 BCE. He ruled for about twenty-five years. Though the king did not campaign as extensively as his father, the evidence from his reign suggests that

Amenhotep II was a ruthless warrior who would hang the bodies of his slain enemies from his ships to instill fear. The Temple of Amun at Karnak features a painting of Amenhotep II smiting foreign prisoners of war. He surrounded himself with advisors from the emerging class of Egyptian military elites, thanks to, in part, personal relations he had developed with many of them during his time in Memphis.

Unlike his father, Amenhotep II was unable to expand the interests of Egypt in the Levant and Mesopotamia, though he was able to protect them. This was largely caused by the weakening of the Mitanni and their inability to keep up the continued war effort against the Egyptians. Ultimately, the balance of power in the region would be disrupted by the re-emergence of the Hittites as a major power in northern Syria, though Egypt was not yet threatened by them during Amenhotep II's reign.

Amenhotep II was succeeded by Thutmose IV around 1400 BCE. The Dream Stela at the front of the Great Sphinx of Giza suggests that he had not been a favored heir. The stela mentions how the king was visited in his sleep by the Sphinx, who promised to make him king if he cleared the sands that had engulfed the body of the figure. Whether he usurped the throne or not, the reign of Thutmose IV brought about the normalization of relations with the Mitanni due to the rising Hittite threat in the north. In fact, the king married the daughter of the Mitanni king, Artatama, establishing an alliance between the two kingdoms.

Overall, Thutmose IV's reign marked a clear break from the expansionist policies of his two predecessors, something that resulted in the weakening of Egyptian influence in Asia but also led to the pharaoh focusing his efforts on developing the temple complexes in his realm. His obelisk, known today as the Lateran Obelisk, which was erected at Karnak, was eventually transported to Rome and placed at the Circus Maximus by Emperor Constantius II in the 4th century CE.

Amenhotep III's rule (c. 1390-1353 BCE) marked the end of the prosperous era. He inherited the throne when he was very young, and it is likely that he ruled with his mother as regent for the first few years of his reign, though this cannot be proven. The king's rule was relatively peaceful, as he only took part in military campaigns in Kush to take control of the gold mines once again. He created policies that strengthened the position of the crown and elevated it to new dimensions of luxury. Ultimately, this resulted in the decline of Egypt's influence in foreign territories, especially in the Levant, where the gains of Thutmose III and other kings were almost completely abandoned.

The focus on domestic affairs may be partially explained by a series of court intrigues that marked Amenhotep III's reign. His Great Royal Wife Tiye would grow her influence in court and in the eyes of the pharaoh. For instance, the king constructed an artificial lake in the city of Akhmim for the queen, showing not only his devotion toward her but also the crown's ability to concentrate so many resources on building projects.

Ultimately, Queen Tiye's strong personality and charm resulted in her representing Egypt in certain foreign affairs. Emissaries and rulers of rival nations were known to have approached the queen, requesting dynastic marriages in exchange for gold. These contacts and alliances did not really impact Egypt's foreign influence. The Hittites convinced the local princes to join them against the Mitanni and the Egyptians.

The efforts to maintain good relations with the Mitanni proved to be futile for Amenhotep III. In fact, it led to the uncontrolled growth of his harem and the development of complex court relationships that created intrigue and weakened the authority of the pharaoh as the supreme decision-maker in the kingdom.

In other respects, Egypt was not troubled during Amenhotep III's reign. A great surplus of gold flowed into Egypt from Nubia. The king recognized this and diverted the funds into building more temple complexes, shrines, royal pavilions, and other monuments throughout Egypt, including in Nubia near the Third Cataract of the Nile. Amenhotep III was well known for the huge mortuary temple he constructed near the city of Luxor; it was the largest ever built in the region up until that point. He also built two sandstone statues, known as the Colossi of Memnon, that are about 65 feet tall and weigh 720 tons. The royal statues of the king and his wife at the sites of Soleb and Sedeinga in Nubia, now in Sudan, were worshiped as divine in their lifetimes. Amenhotep III also commissioned the making of hundreds of statues of the lion goddess Sckhmet, the daughter of Ra. The prestige of the crown and the grandiosity of the court were revived during Amenhotep III's reign.

The Colossi of Memnon in the 19th century.[5]

Akhenaten and the Late Eighteenth Dynasty

Amenhotep III died in 1353 BCE from an illness he had wrestled with for months. He was succeeded by his son, Amenhotep IV, who became one of the most compelling and notorious figures in history. He had served as his father's co-ruler for quite some time, and the first few years of his sole rule did not stray too much from the traditional pharaonic activities. However, Amenhotep IV became one of the most disliked pharaohs in Egyptian history.

Even ancient Egyptians reversed most of his policies and did not include him in the king lists. This was because Amenhotep IV is considered to have been the first recorded ruler to endorse monotheistic beliefs, elevating the deity Aten to the position of the supreme god in the Egyptian pantheon. The result was a brief but radical transformation of the ancient Egyptian cultural, social, and political order. It had never been seen before.

The story of how Amenhotep IV transformed Egypt from a place with one of the most diverse pantheons to a monotheistic society is interesting. There is no evidence to suggest that this had been a pre-planned move to accrue more power and control or that it was done in the interests of other actors. From what we know, Amenhotep IV gradually began to show his devotion toward Aten, the deity represented as the sun disk, which had been personally preferred by him, not his royal parents. Egyptian pharaohs had always been associated with the worship of the sun due to the popularity of Ra, and it seems that Aten was viewed by the king as a manifestation of Ra. The king constructed a temple devoted to Aten at Karnak, which was traditionally a site for the worship of Amun. The temple featured art with completely new designs. For instance, the statues depicting the pharaoh were no longer idealistic and aesthetic in shape and form. Instead, they portrayed the king in a more unconventional, expressive, and realistic manner, with a large stomach, thick thighs, and thick hips.

This feminine depiction of the king stemmed from the understanding that the pharaoh was both the father and mother of his subjects as the representative of god on earth. However, the decision to actually sculpt the pharaoh's statue in this way was entirely new.

This went hand in hand with the gradual replacement of traditional depictions of chief deities with depictions of Aten. The transformation represented the idea that Aten was the creator of all and that he manifested this position by reaching all with the sun's rays. As the sole possessor of such divinity, Aten was perceived to be the ruler of all creatures, and it is only natural that Sed festivals were celebrated in his name; traditionally, Sed festivals were only organized to mark thirty years of a pharaoh's rule.

Having surrounded himself with a trusted group of individuals and having dismissed his father's court, Amenhotep IV began to slowly enforce this understanding of Aten as the supreme deity and to completely reorganize Egypt's society and culture. Two things symbolized the transformation of the existing social order.

Amarna art.⁶

    The first was the founding of the new capital at a previously uninhabited site, about halfway between two of the most important cities in Egypt, Memphis and Thebes. The ancient Egyptian name of the new city was Akhetaten, which means "horizon of Aten." It has come to be known as Amarna due to the local Bedouin tribes who eventually came to inhabit it. Amarna was a stunning project, complete with royal palaces and temples. Its borders were marked with inscribed stelae that spoke about the might of Aten. The city became the center of worship of Aten, as well as the residence of the king and his inner court. Most of the state officials continued to reside in other cities.

The second decision Amenhotep IV made that emphasizes the transition Egypt underwent during this time was the change of the pharaoh's name to Akhenaten. It is easy to assume that this was a conscious break from the past. The ruler's previous name meant "Amun is pleased," which was an allusion to the god Amun, who was slowly being replaced as the chief Egyptian deity. The king no longer wanted to be associated with him.

These events marked the beginning of a cultural and political revolution. Akhenaten and his allies radically transformed the social landscape of ancient Egypt. After settling in Amarna, the king ordered the complete erasure of any evidence that pointed to older Egyptian beliefs. Names, depictions, and statues of all deities other than Aten were destroyed throughout the kingdom's numerous temples and altars. The cult of Amun was especially targeted. It was desecrated the most due to its significance and recent association with the pharaoh.

This was one of the first well-documented instances of iconoclasm (the destruction of religious and symbolic imagery for political reasons) in ancient history. At the same time, the king financed the modification of the existing temples as places of worship exclusively for Aten, and the deity was given paramount importance.

Aten received a new title and was officially endorsed as the only god that could be worshiped. Akhenaten was the chief promulgator of the new belief, which has rightfully been called the first recorded monotheistic religion in history. The pharaoh forced his subjects to accept the new faith, and most people obliged, though there is evidence of them still following the old beliefs and practices privately in the safety of their homes. Publicly, however, they accepted that there was only one god and that King Akhenaten was the sole mediator between the divine and the earthly. The royal family, King Akhenaten and his wife, Nefertiti, were depicted on altar walls engulfed in the rays of the sun disk.

While Akhenaten was busy reinventing the Egyptian belief system and enforcing monotheism on his subjects, the conquests of his predecessors in the Levant were slowly slipping from his control. This is attested to by the Amarna letters, an archive of clay tablet letters between the Egyptian administration in the new capital and diplomats and political leaders in the Levant. The letters contain valuable information about the ongoing political situation in the region, including pleas for help from the Canaanite princes, who requested aid from Akhenaten against foreign invaders.

One of the Amarna letters'

Akhenaten virtually neglected his duties as king, as he was occupied by his ambitious remodeling of the Egyptian religion. He left foreign policy affairs to his officials. This resulted in the declining influence of Egypt in western Asia. Many important cities were lost to the rising influence of the Hittites or to the emerging Amorite Kingdom. These two regional powers slowly picked off the Canaanite territories that had been left alone. The main ally of Egypt, the Kingdom of Mitanni, was also eclipsed, resulting in a total reversal of gains in the region.

The final years of Akhenaten's reign are just as interesting and filled with mystery. We know that the Great Royal Wife Nefertiti bore the king six daughters but no sons, which created complications when it came to succession. A person by the name of Smenkhkare appears briefly as the next pharaoh, though we don't really know who this person was or even his gender. It is generally accepted that Smenkhkare was a close ally and son-in-law of Akhenaten, married to the princess Meritaten. Smenkhkare most likely took over control around 1335 BCE, right after the death of Akhenaten, and built a mortuary temple at Thebes.

What complicates things further is evidence of another ruler at around the same time by the name of Neferneferuaten, who is believed to have been female. It is thought she was either Nefertiti or Meritaten. There is evidence that Queen Nefertiti had been disfavored by the end of Akhenaten's reign, so the theory of the Great Royal Wife "exacting her revenge" on his subjects by ascending the throne is plausible. Whatever the case, by the year 1333 BCE, Akhenaten had been dead for a couple of years, resulting in a brief succession crisis, which would only be solved by the accession of Tutankhaten.

At the time of his accession, Tutankhaten was very young. Egypt was ruled by his regent Ay, one of the most important viziers during Akhenaten's reign. Ay appears to have been a wise person, a typical example of someone who served the state and not any particular ruler. He began to adopt a policy that saw Egypt slowly move away from the radical shifts caused during the Amarna period. His aim was to peacefully restore the old order. Amarna was abandoned as the capital, and it was moved back to Memphis. The break from the monotheistic rule of Akhenaten was manifested by the name change of the pharaoh from Tutankhaten to Tutankhamun. Though this meant the return to the cult of Amun, it was by no means a radical reaction to the changes implemented by Akhenaten. Old temples dedicated to Amun began to be restored, and the temples of Aten were largely left intact.

Tutankhamun's short reign, which lasted until circa 1323 to 1322 BCE, was otherwise insignificant. Yes, it was the beginning of the reversal of Akhenaten's monotheistic policies, but Tutankhamun was not considered to have been a great king by later Egyptians, leading to the omission of his name from later king lists. This partially had to do with the pharaoh's early death, which was most likely from complications after contracting malaria. He was already in poor health when he contracted malaria. Tutankhamun died without an heir and was buried in a relatively modest tomb in the Valley of Kings. The location of his burial was forgotten over time.

Nevertheless, Tutankhamun is one of the most recognizable names from ancient Egypt. This is because of the famous discovery of his tomb by English archaeologist Howard Carter in 1922. The tomb managed to largely survive tomb robbers, who had plagued the pharaonic burial sites for centuries. The tomb, full of decorations, valuables, and lavish ornaments, provided little insight into Tutankhamun's reign, but it was a great example of the luxury ancient Egyptian pharaohs enjoyed. The king's mummy lay in three coffins, the innermost being made of solid gold. Tutankhamun's sarcophagus and his death mask also feature inlays of gold and other valuable materials.

Opening of Tutankhamun's tomb.*

The death of Tutankhamun resulted in a succession crisis. The pharaoh had left no male heirs, leading to the kingdom being ruled for the next several years by members of his court. Ay, Tutankhamun's vizier, ascended the throne around 1323 BCE and ruled for no more than four years, during which time he tried to drag Egypt out of its passivity in foreign and security policies, something that had begun during the reign of Akhenaten. With the help of Horemheb, a prominent military general, he was able to eliminate any opposition to his claim. Ay made the general his designated successor early on, as he himself was already very old.

Horemheb came from a non-royal background and would rule Egypt for around the next fourteen years. He would later be regarded as the restorer of peace and stability in the realm due to his influential policies that were concerned with a total reversal of the changes adopted during the Amarna period. During Horemheb's reign, systematic persecution of the Amarna kings, mainly Akhenaten and, to a lesser degree, Tutankhamun and Ay, began. The king tore down the temples dedicated to Aten and tried to erase the memory of the deity that had turned Egyptian society upside down.

The fight against Atenism included imprisoning or exiling the cult's priests. Horemheb also tried to revitalize the cult of Amun, visiting Thebes every year despite the fact that his residence was in Memphis and contributing to the expansion of the temple complex at Karnak. The Amarna period was subsequently instilled in the memory of ancient Egyptians as a shameful era, as it was a time when Egypt lost its international prestige and power due to the obsessions of a single ruler.

The Nineteenth Dynasty

By the early 13th century BCE, ancient Egypt had been ruled by a succession of eighteen royal dynasties. The Amarna period had been a unique time during this era, lasting for only a few decades but significantly impacting Egyptian society and culture. It brought about a sense of longing for the "good old times." There was a definite need to rebuild Egypt and bring it back to its former glory.

Before his death, Horemheb appointed his vizier and a veteran military commander by the name of Paramessu as his successor. Ascending the throne circa 1292 BCE, Paramessu ruled as Ramesses I for the next two years, laying the foundations for the Nineteenth Dynasty. He ruled for too short a time to leave a lasting impact, and his reign is mostly regarded as a necessary transition period back to dynastic rule where succession was determined by blood. Two years later, his son, Seti I (c. 1290–1279 BCE), would inherit the Egyptian throne.

Known as Sethos I to the Greeks, the new pharaoh had a lot of work to do if he wanted to meet the expectations bestowed upon him. Reestablishing the pre-Amarna order was still the highest goal on the agenda. One of the ways this was achieved was by increasing the importance of some of the oldest Egyptian deities. Named after the deity Seth, a central figure in the Egyptian pantheon that had been especially worshiped by the Hyksos, Seti I built a temple to the god in the northern part of the kingdom, resulting in Seth regaining its importance as a chief deity alongside Amun, Ptah, and Ra.

Seti I, who ruled from Memphis, launched several military campaigns in western Asia to challenge the emerging Hittite Empire in control of the valuable region. The first campaign into the Levant served to reestablish Egyptian control over the military routes that connected Egypt to the Sinai Peninsula. This meant they had to defeat the local Bedouin tribes, which were a thorn in the side of the Egyptian armies. The king followed this up by capturing the important city of Kadesh, which had been lost during Akhenaten's reign. Seti I erected a stela commemorating his victory there. The son of Seti I and the future king of Egypt, Ramesses II, accompanied the pharaoh during this campaign. The pharaoh also conducted military operations against the invading Libyan tribes in the western part of his realm and quelled a rebellion in Nubia, though he might not have personally led his forces in these endeavors. These military activities served to revitalize the long-standing military tradition of Egypt, shifting the focus back to the pragmatic foreign policy of the early New Kingdom rulers.

Perhaps the most successful of all of Egypt's rulers was Ramesses II. He ascended the throne in 1279 BCE and ruled for the next sixty-six years, making him the second longest-ruling pharaoh in Egyptian history after Pepi II. Ramesses II is one of those rulers who are known as "the great." The young Ramesses had been involved in state affairs very early on, enjoying all of the benefits of being a crown prince. He was the designated successor for a long time. There is still an ongoing debate about whether or not Ramesses II was actually made a full-on co-ruler by his father, but regardless, he demonstrated his enthusiasm and aptness to rule early on.

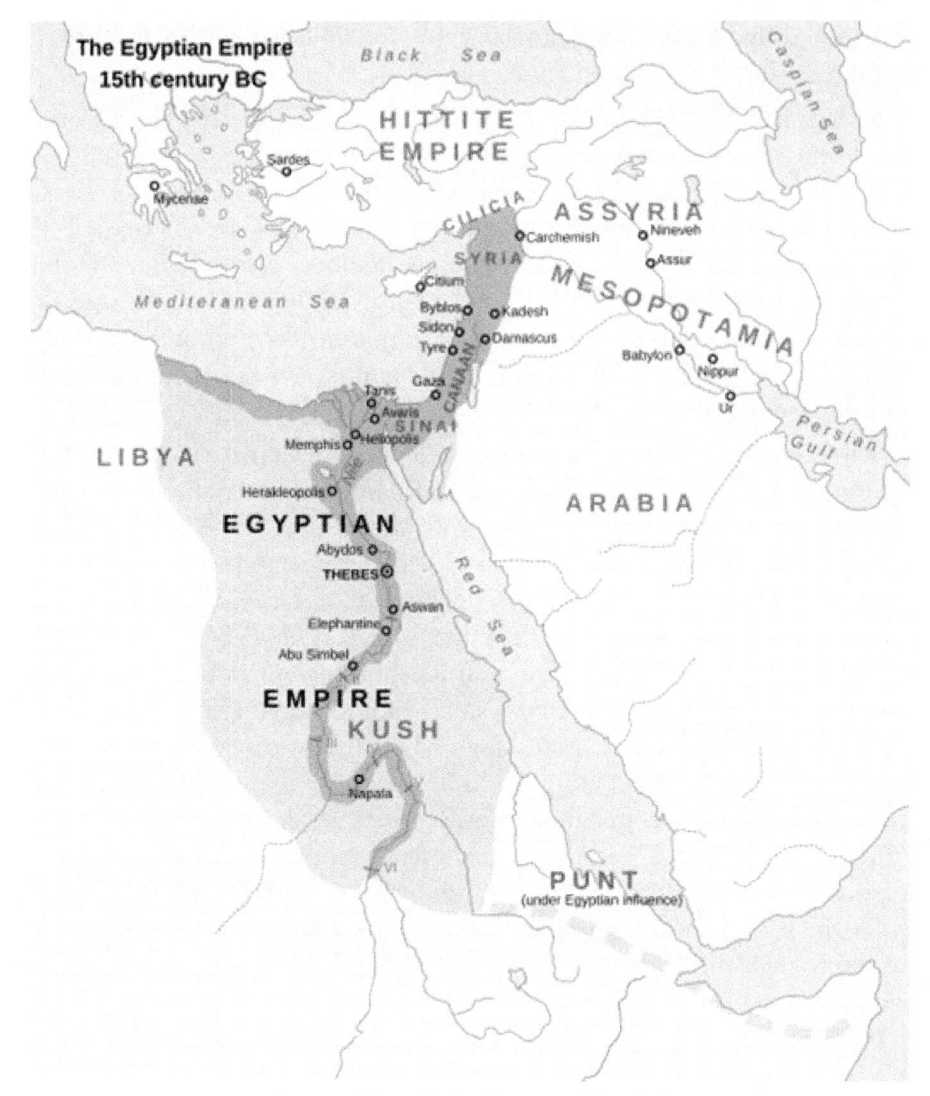

A map of Egypt during Ramesses II's rule.⁹

One of the new pharaoh's first decisions was to expand his father's royal residence in Lower Egypt near Qantir in the eastern delta. The residence would ultimately be remodified into a full city, which would house over 200,000 inhabitants at its peak. Known as Pi-Ramesses or the "House of Ramesses," it was equipped with a large palace and royal quarters, temples, and lavish decorations, such as sphinxes and statues of Egyptian deities and kings. Once the site was up and running, most of Ramesses II's administration would eventually move there from Memphis, making Pi-Ramesses the center of Egyptian politics.

When it came to foreign policy, the achievements of Ramesses II were not as impressive as those of his predecessor, Thutmose III, who expanded Egypt's borders to its farthest extent. However, this is partially because the enemies Ramesses II had to face in western Asia were much better organized and prepared for the Egyptians. The pharaoh's main goal was to secure Egypt's borders and sphere of influence against the Hittite Empire, and this goal was achieved very quickly.

Before the king even organized an offensive into the Levant against the Hittites, Ramesses II first defeated the Mediterranean Sea pirates known as the Sherden, who had terrorized the Egyptian coast. Unbeknownst to the pharaoh, the Sherden were one of the groups of the semi-legendary Sea Peoples who would become prominent during the 11th century BCE. They brought about the decline of many Mediterranean civilizations during the Late Bronze Age Collapse.

Ramesses II first campaigned into the Levant during the fourth year of his reign, and he was successful in taking the old territories of the Amorite Kingdom. This campaign extended the Egyptian sphere of influence back to the city of Ugarit, something that did not go unnoticed by the Hittites, who saw the Egyptian advances as an infringement on their own interests.

The pharaoh, just like his father, erected a victory stela at Nahr el-Kalb near modern-day Beirut, Lebanon. The Hittites, led by King Muwatalli II, decided to retaliate. He assembled a large force and waited for Ramesses II's forces near Kadesh, where the two armies engaged in one of the most important battles of the ancient world: the Battle of Kadesh.

The Battle of Kadesh, which took place in May 1274 BCE, has caused great debate among historians. Records from both sides mention the course of the battle and its aftermath, leading to the existence of conflicting accounts. While we don't have an exact number of the forces that fought at Kadesh, it is believed that the strength of the two armies was roughly equal at about twenty thousand to forty thousand men each. It also appears that Muwatalli II got the upper hand at first, catching Ramesses' forces off-guard by a sudden chariot attack before the Egyptians knew they had been marching into battle. This greatly disorganized the Egyptian army, which had to fight the rest of the skirmish on the back foot. After heavy casualties, both sides claimed victory. Today, the Battle of Kadesh is considered to have ended in a stalemate.

Though Egyptian sources mention the Hittite forces had to flee beyond the nearby Orontes River to the north, Ramesses realized that his army in no condition to continue the campaign. He returned to Egypt and recouped his losses, relaunching many offensives in the Levant during the next few years.

After sporadic fighting, which did not result in the change of the status quo in the region and took a heavy toll on the resources of both kings, the two sides finally struck a peace treaty around 1259 BCE—more than fifteen years after the Battle of Kadesh. The peace treaty was concluded after mediation between Ramesses II and Hittite King Hattusili III. The treaty has been preserved in both Egyptian and Akkadian. According to the document, both nations had to stop waging wars against each other and work together to preserve the status quo. Kadesh fell into the Hittites' sphere of influence, while the land of the Amurru belonged to Egypt, marking the boundary between the two powers in the Levant.

This treaty is the earliest known international treaty. Though both sides respected the agreement and proceeded to uphold it immediately after striking the deal, the rivalry between Egypt and the Hittite Empire did not end. However, Ramesses II, recognizing the importance of a secure northeastern border, cultivated closer personal ties with the Hittites, leading to the eventual alliance between the two kingdoms. The Egyptian pharaoh married the daughter of the Hittite king in 1245 BCE, and it is not unlikely that he married another princess later on. He probably visited Canaan again after the deal had been struck and was glad to send King Hattusili Egyptian physicians when the latter suffered an illness.

Relations between Egypt and Anatolians were normalized and based on a mutual understanding of the need for peace and prosperity. A copy of the peace treaty is always on display at the United Nations Headquarters in New York, symbolizing the millennia-long tradition of finding international solutions through mediation.

The campaigns in the Levant and the treaty with the Hittites secured much-needed peace for Ramesses II. It also secured control over the lucrative trade routes that ran through the region and deep into Asia, which brought great economic gains for Egypt. The king also campaigned in the gold-rich Nubian territories south of the First Cataract of the Nile. Thanks to a series of defensive structures along the northwestern coast of Egypt along the Mediterranean, the North African Libyan tribes were kept in check.

Secure borders meant that full attention could be devoted to domestic development, something that was recognized by Ramesses II, who built extensively over the course of his reign. The abundance of building projects commissioned by Ramesses II is one of the best markers of economic and political prosperity enjoyed by the pharaoh during his long reign.

Traces of Ramesses II's extensive building projects can be found all over Egypt and Nubia. He constructed temples and altars at all of the major cultural sites of ancient Egypt. At Abu Simbel, he cut two huge temples in the rock, complete with giant statues on the exterior that marvel visitors to this day. Ramesses II completed his father's tomb and expanded the Karnak complex. His own mortuary temple, Ramesseum, is located at the Theban necropolis. It reflects the grandeur of the king and symbolizes the prosperity and power of Egypt during his rule. Grandiosity was certainly the main characteristic of the art and architecture produced during the reign of Ramesses II.

The Ramesseum features elegant and chunky columns, intricate and deeper reliefs depicting the king and his actions, and massive statues of Ramesses alongside some of Egypt's most important deities. The king also transformed many of the older temples of importance at some of the most prominent sites in Egypt, such as Abydos and Thebes. He restored and modified the relief works of many of these temples and even inscribed them with his cartouches (hieroglyphs that denoted royal status) despite the fact that he had not constructed them. The projects commissioned by the king feature artistic and literary accounts of some of the most important events that transpired during Ramesses II's reign, something that served to magnify the status of the king and his achievements.

The façade of the Abu Simbel temple, taken in 2019.[10]

These projects provide valuable insights into Ramesses the Great's reign. Egypt reached the peak of its prosperity during his tenure as pharaoh, bouncing back from the troublesome era of the Amarna period. The genius of Ramesses II and his ability to adapt to the changing political circumstances around him are best manifested in the peace treaty with the Hittites. Ramesses II was a ruler who knew and worked toward addressing the needs of his realm, rightfully claiming his successes that resulted in one of the golden eras of ancient Egypt. The gains made by this pharaoh would last for a long time, though ancient Egypt would never again see the emergence of such a powerful and influential ruler.

The Fall of the New Kingdom

Ramesses II had an unusually large number of children, but pretty much the only thing we know of them is their names. His harem was also unusually large, consisting of many wives and concubines, leading to confusion when it comes to the royal lineage. Merneptah, the thirteenth child of the king, ascended the throne at an old age in 1213 BCE and ruled for the next decade. Favoring the deity Ptah, as can be observed from his name, the new king decided to abandon the Pi-Ramesses royal residence and moved back to Memphis, where the cult of Ptah was the strongest.

His reign was significant, as it marked the continuation of Egypt's struggles against the Sea Peoples. In addition to the Sherden, who had already been beaten back by Ramesses II, other peoples like the Tursha, the Luka, and the Shekelesh launched an attack on northwestern Egypt, having struck an alliance with the Libyans. The attack, which came in 1208, was defeated by Merneptah. The decline of the Nineteenth Dynasty is usually thought to have begun with his death.

Merneptah's son and successor, Seti II, had to face an open rebellion upon his accession to the throne circa 1203 BCE. He was challenged by a man named Amenmesse, who, according to some historians, was Seti II's half-brother or even a son of Ramesses II. Having acted as a viceroy of Nubia, Amenmesse launched a military campaign against the new king, leading his rebellion down the Nile River to the north. Ultimately, he was defeated by King Seti II and was deemed a usurper, but the situation did not instantly stabilize. It is also possible that Amenmesse recouped his power and claimed to be the king for a few months in 1197 BCE, maybe even taking part in the pharaoh's death around the same time. Meanwhile, the Sea Peoples began regular assaults on the eastern Mediterranean societies, leading to the destruction of many cities in the Levant, as well as the Hittite Empire itself.

In an increasingly complicated political climate, Seti II's son, Siptah, ascended the throne. He was still too young to rule himself in 1197 BCE. The real power lay in the hands of his mother, Tausret, who would only rule as a sole ruler for two years, beginning in 1190 BCE. Much like Hatshepsut, she assumed the full royal titles and was buried in a carefully designed tomb in the Valley of Kings. The queen might have also shared power with a man named Bay, an official of Syrian origin who was buried by Tausret's tomb. Material evidence implies that, at one time, Siptah, Tausret, and Bay were all considered to have been equal rulers of the kingdom, though it is difficult to speculate. In any case, Tausret was the last ruler of the Nineteenth Dynasty.

The events that transpired in the later stages of Tausret's rule are unclear, but it is very likely that another succession crisis erupted around 1190 BCE. A man by the name of Setnakht assumed power and established the Twentieth Dynasty of Egypt after supposedly eliminating the opposition to his reign. There are several theories about the motivations behind Setnakht's actions. We are unsure whether he was an established official during the reign of Tausret who rebelled against the pharaoh or whether he faced a lot of challenges after power was peacefully transferred to him. What we do know is that the new pharaoh recognized Seti II as the last legitimate ruler of Egypt. Interestingly, many historians trace the roots of this confusion back to the many children of Ramesses II, which resulted in the development of many interrelated branches of the royal house.

Setnakht's son, Ramesses III, is considered to be the last significant ruler of the New Kingdom, ruling for about thirty years, from around 1186 to 1155 BCE. Ramesses III saw Ramesses the Great as the most important Egyptian king and believed himself to have been his successor. He imitated the Nineteenth Dynasty ruler when it came to his deeds, celebrating some of his major achievements, such as the Battle of Kadesh, which was considered to have been a great Egyptian victory by ancient Egyptians. Much like Ramesses II and Merneptah, Ramesses III had to deal with foreign threats at his borders, including the Sea Peoples and the Libyans, who attacked Egypt multiple times during his reign. The Libyans were defeated on two separate occasions, in 1182 and 1176 BCE, while the Sea Peoples were barely held off at the Nile Delta in 1179 BCE. These victories provided Ramesses III with much-needed security for the rest of his reign. Many soldiers were taken prisoners and were either resettled to foreign lands, such as the Levant, or integrated into the Egyptian army.

Ramesses III imitated Ramesses II in his extensive building projects. He constructed several temples at Thebes and expanded the Karnak complex. He also built his own grandiose mortuary temple at Medinet Habu, located near the modern-day city of Luxor. However, unlike his namesake, Ramesses III's reign suffered a series of social and economic difficulties that marked the beginning of the decline of the Twentieth Dynasty. Economic problems were caused by the expenses that had to be spent to defend the kingdom's borders from invaders. Historians also believe that Ramesses III's reign coincided with sudden changes in the climate, which temporarily affected agricultural production, leading to food shortages throughout Egypt. Material and written evidence attests to the problems faced by Ramesses III.

At the very end of his reign, Ramesses III had to deal with the disenchanted working-class population of the village Deir el-Medina, whose dwellers were artisans and craftsmen who worked on the lucrative royal building projects in Thebes. Shortage of supplies and tough working conditions resulted in the first-ever recorded labor strike in history. The people of Deir el-Medina complained to the administration about their problems and refused to go back to work unless their needs were met.

What ultimately caused the downfall of Ramesses III was a court conspiracy, which we know about thanks to the Turin legal papyrus, which was produced by the king's court during the trial of the conspirators. According to the document, late into his reign, the royal harem of King Ramesses plotted a coup d'état with the intention of overthrowing the pharaoh. The conspiracy was led by Tiye, a secondary wife of the king, who probably wished to install her son, Pentawer, on the throne. Scholarly opinion is still divided on the matter, but it is likely that the conspirators succeeded in killing the king or at least managed to weaken him considerably. However, they were unable to install a preferred candidate to the throne. This meant that the designated successor and son of the king, Ramesses IV, ascended the throne around 1155 BCE, condemning the conspirators, who were either put to death or mutilated as a form of punishment.

Eight successive rulers of Egypt's Twentieth Dynasty were called Ramesses, and their reigns were short-lived. Ramesses IV, who ruled for about seven years, attempted to replicate the grandiosity of Ramesses II's building projects, sending thousands of workers to the mines of Wadi Hammamat. His reign produced the Harris Papyrus, the longest surviving papyrus from ancient Egypt, which tells the history of the realm under Ramesses III. He would be succeeded by Ramesses V in 1148 BCE, who died at an early age from smallpox in 1143 BCE.

Ramesses VI, who ruled for the next eight years, was most likely the son of Ramesses III, something that can be deduced by his old age by the time he became pharaoh. The Wilbour Papyrus, which dates from this time, is an important document that captures the socioeconomic situation of Egypt. It is an administrative document that contains sections related to the existing cultivatable land and its ownership by people of different professions and classes. According to the Wilbour Papyrus, the religious officials of Egypt were amongst the most numerous landholders in the society. This foreshadowed the eventual rise of the religious elite, who would slowly emerge as the most dominant strata and gain hold of the political power in the kingdom.

The decline of the pharaoh's power was already evident by this time. The lack of written evidence is a characteristic of chaotic and unstable times, and it is partially because of this that we know little about the decisions of the pharaohs during this time. Economic and social troubles put great pressure on the later pharaohs of the Twentieth Dynasty. There was an increasing number of tomb robberies, something that was caused by the lack of maintenance of the royal tombs. Some members of society, like the laborers of Deir el-Medina, organized strikes under Ramesses X (c. 1108-1104 BCE). Pharaonic authority was slowly being eclipsed by the rising religious elite, while the distant dependencies of the kingdom were becoming increasingly independent. This caused the formation of internal political disputes that would characterize Egypt for the next few centuries.

Ramesses XI (c. 1104-1075 BCE) was the final ruler of the Twentieth Dynasty. The king would be unable to reverse the declining course of the kingdom. Unexpected ecological factors resulted in an increasing number of floods and food shortages, putting pressure on the socioeconomic situation. Growing political tensions put further constraints on the pharaoh, who could only watch the meteoric rise in the religious elites' power in Thebes, as well as the increasing dissatisfaction of his southern vassals. Egypt's dependencies in the Levant had either broken free or been absorbed by the rising Assyrian Empire, which would dominate its rivals in the Near East.

By the year 1082 BCE, it is believed that the real power lay in the hands of Smendes, who was most likely married to the pharaoh's daughter. He would eventually move the capital to the city of Tanis and become the founder of the Twenty-first Dynasty of Egypt, though his rule never extended beyond Lower Egypt. Upper and Middle Egypt would be increasingly dominated by the priesthood of Amun, which would translate its religious influence into political power by the end of the Twentieth Dynasty.

The Third Intermediate Period

The fall of the Twentieth Dynasty ushered in the Third Intermediate Period, which, much like its predecessors, was marked by political and social turmoil. Egypt was divided by the power groups that had emerged by the late Twentieth Dynasty; this situation would last until the 7th century BCE. In the north, Smendes and his successors ruled as the Twenty-first Dynasty until around 950 BCE. It is also referred to as the Tanite dynasty because they ruled from the city of Tanis. The southern parts of the realm were firmly under the control of the Theban priestly class, which came from the cult of Amun and had slowly grown their material wealth and gained ownership of more lands.

Nominally, the Twenty-first Dynasty kings were kings of all of Egypt, and they were not technically challenged by the religious elite in the south. Documents from the era are dated according to the chronology of the Tanite kings, something that attests to the lack of a direct conflict between the two. Some of the Theban priests assumed the royal titles and ruled as kings during this period but only after their "kingship" or rather "overlordship" was recognized by Tanis. In practice, however, the extent of their power was limited up to the city of Tayu-djayet, now known as El Hiba, which marked a frontier between the two power bases.

Map of Egypt during the Third Intermediate Period.[11]

Though the Third Intermediate Period is ultimately considered to be a transitory stage, it includes many interesting domestic political developments that we should examine to understand their impact on the Late Period of Egypt. Due to the rising influence of the Theban priesthood, the deity Amun was back on top of the Egyptian pantheon. This was true not only for Upper Egypt, which was ruled by priests, but also for the Tanite dynasty, which made efforts to remodel Tanis after Thebes. Amun was generally regarded to have been the "ruler" of Egypt at the time or at least the divine source of legitimacy for the rulers. Unlike the Middle and New Kingdom eras, where the notion of kingship was gradually infused with divine elements and became a supreme institution, the Third Intermediate Period saw great reversals when it came to the understanding of this concept. Not only did the regime have a prominent theocratic element, but it was also composed of military elites. It is also possible that members of the two ruling classes were related to each other, something that contributed to the mutual understanding of the division of Egyptian lands.

There was a general decline in the ambitious building projects. This was mostly because the Twenty-first Dynasty kings did not have the same resources available to them as their predecessors. Both the Theban priests and the Tanite royals were more concerned with preserving and renovating many of the older royal temples and tombs.

This is why the reign of King Siamun of the Twenty-first Dynasty (c. 978--960 BCE) is considered to be significant. The king supposedly led his forces into the Levant, taking the Philistine city of Gezer from the newly emergent Kingdom of Israel. Interestingly, his daughter would later enter the harem of King Solomon of Israel in an act to stabilize the relations between the two kingdoms. The recently captured city of Gezer was included in the princess's dowry and was returned back to the Israelites.

The second half of the 10th century BCE marked the end of the Twenty-first Dynasty and the establishment, for the first time in centuries, of a dynasty that was not of Egyptian origin. Libyan war chieftains had been increasingly employed by the Egyptian kings in their armies since the Twentieth Dynasty. This stemmed from the necessity to keep the western borders of the kingdom safe, something that could only be achieved if the Libyan leaders were integrated to some degree into the prosperous Egyptian society. Under Psusennes II (c. 960–945 BCE), who is considered to have been both a pharaoh of the Twenty-first Dynasty and the high priest of Amun, the influence of the Libyan mercenaries eclipsed the king's power.

Having allied themselves with the Theban priests through marriage, one of the Libyan war chiefs by the name of Nimlot managed to increase his power base in Lower Egypt. His son, Shoshenq I (943-922 BCE), is considered to be the founder of the Libyan Twenty-second Dynasty. He secured both parts of the kingdom through inheritance and interpersonal relations. He was succeeded by his son Osorkon I, whose bust with royal inscriptions was discovered in the city of Byblos in the Levant.

Osorkon I then installed his son, Shoshenq, as the high priest of Amun, signifying the shift in the power relations that had happened in Egypt with the advent of the Libyan rulers, who enforced their rule through a strong military that even campaigned into the Levant. King Osorkon I ruled until around 887 BCE, and he would be buried alongside his son, who was either made a co-ruler in the later years of his reign or briefly usurped the throne before dying at around the same time.

The Libyan kings of Egypt experienced many problems during their reigns. Their complicated lineage and taking of different Egyptian lands resulted in the rise of locally recognized rulers who were sometimes the descendants of the same family. This caused confusion and further weakened the authority of the king, who was technically still at Tanis and appointed the rulers of these local areas despite being unable to control them. Over time, the power base of the Twenty-second Dynasty kings was reduced to a small portion of the Nile Delta in Lower Egypt. Upper Egypt became politically decentralized.

This fragmentation continued after the death of King Osorkon III (c. 787-759 BCE), whose son, Takelot III, was installed in Thebes as the next king. He faced increasing pressure from the rulers of Herakleopolis and Hermopolis in the north, who had established hereditary rule over their domains and defied the orders of the pharaoh. Lower Egypt was completely divided between rival houses and cities, something that would last until the eventual reunification by King Psamtik I in the second half of the 7th century BCE.

The decline of royal authority and the collapse of centralized rule in Egypt resulted in the decline of Tanis. Sais in the western delta of the Nile became the new political center. Its ruler, Tefnakht (c. 732-725 BCE), who is also considered to be the first of the two rulers of the short-lived Twenty-fourth Dynasty, managed to briefly conquer Memphis and attacked Heracleopolis. His advance was checked by a new challenger of foreign origins.

The Kushites had emerged as a potential political rival to Egypt by the middle of the 8th century BCE. The Kingdom of Kush, whose King Kashta had managed to solidify the power base around the cities of Napata and Meroe, eventually came to control much of Upper Egypt and was recognized as such in Thebes. His son, Piye (Piankhi), would lead the Kushite forces to the north, conquering the territories along the way and receiving submission from the local rulers.

The Kushites were of Nubian descent, but they regarded themselves as Egyptians, as they practiced the Egyptian religion and followed other aspects of Egyptian culture. This is unsurprising given the influence and the heavy presence of Egypt in Nubia, which would have resulted in the appropriation of many Egyptian practices. During the Eighteenth Dynasty, the Temple of Amun was built at Napata, resulting in the Kushites worshiping the deity and attributing as much importance to him as the Egyptians from the Third Intermediate Period.

Upon the unification of their kingdom and advancement into Egypt, the Kushites tried to imitate the old practices of the "real" Egyptian rulers as much as possible, even erecting pyramids in Napata for their royals. When Piye achieved the victory against Tefnakht, he erected a victory stela, on which he boasted about his "Egyptian origins" and talked about his campaign in the politically unstable north.

In a compelling turn of events, the spirit of the Egyptian civilization was defended by an Egyptianized Kushite king, who established control over southern Egypt. The Kushites took over Thebes and allowed the local cult of Amun to continue its activities undisturbed.

In the north, the situation looked much more fragmented. The cities of Herakleopolis, Hermopolis, and Memphis all used the title of king, though the descendants of the Libyan dynasty ruled from the latter. Nevertheless, these rulers were no match for King Piye, who accepted the submission of the northern Egyptian rulers. He watched as the petty kings of the delta tried to challenge the might of the Assyrian Empire under Sargon II, who had conquered Israel and threatened the eastern border of Egypt. In 720 BCE, the Egyptians were defeated by Sargon in a battle in modern-day Palestine. King Bocchoris, son of Tefnakht, is considered to be the second of the two rulers of the short-lived Libyan Twenty-fourth Dynasty. The Kushites, under Piye's brother and successor Shabaka (712-

698 BCE), once again campaigned to the north after his accession and managed to defeat the Lower Egyptian rulers once again, burning Bocchoris alive.

Under Shabaka and his successors, the influence of older Egyptian artistic and architectural styles once again became evident. Thanks to the control of the Nubian gold mines, the Kushite kings were able to invest heavily in the economic revitalization of the war-torn Egyptian lands. King Taharqa, who succeeded Shabaka circa 690 BCE, constructed extensively during his reign. He built up the temple complexes of Amun at both Karnak and Thebes. In the latter, he established a marriage alliance with the local priesthood of Amun, something that allowed him to effectively exercise control over the important city. His reign unexpectedly saw the largest recorded inundation of the Nile in centuries, leading to economic and social disruptions that added to Egypt's troubles. Interestingly, the Egyptians saw this as a manifestation of the divine. As it was so unnatural and impactful, it had to be attributed to otherworldly reasons.

King Taharqa's reign was also challenged by Assyrian King Esarhaddon, who invaded northern Egypt in the later years of the 670s and eventually managed to push to Memphis with his army. Taharqa was forced to relocate southward as the northern rulers of the delta allied themselves with the foreigners. Taharqa was able to briefly regain the city, holding it for a couple of years until around 667 BCE but had to relinquish it after Esarhaddon's successor, King Ashurbanipal, organized his own offensive into Egypt. Ashurbanipal bestowed the title of "lesser king" on the Libyan ruler Necho I, who essentially became his puppet in the destabilized Egyptian realm. Taharqa was forced to flee to Thebes and then to Napata, where he died around 664 BCE.

The reunification of Thebes would occur under King Psamtik I of Sais, the founder of the Twenty-sixth Dynasty who ruled for over fifty years. His reign inaugurated the so-called Late Period of ancient Egyptian history, which would last for about the next three hundred years. Supported by the Assyrians, who considered him their puppet in the north, Psamtik was able to consolidate his control over fragmented Lower Egypt before advancing farther to the south and taking Thebes in 656 BCE. The king was able to achieve his victories thanks to the help of soldiers from the distant Kingdom of Lydia, which considered Egypt a potential ally against its main rival, the Assyrian Empire.

Psamtik was finally able to stabilize the domestic situation in Egypt after decades of infighting, and he waited for an opportune moment for expansion. Due to the large influx of Greek immigrants from Lydia and Caria, important developments took place in the Egyptian religion. The cult of Amun declined in importance. Instead, the cult of Osiris was promoted alongside many of the other deities associated with his mythology, including Isis and Serapis, the two gods who would increasingly emerge as central figures of the Egyptian pantheon.

In addition, Psamtik I's armies became increasingly composed of foreign legions. They came not only from Greece but also from Libya, a region with a long tradition of producing strong mercenary corps, as well as from Phoenicia and Palestine. The intermingling of thousands of people from all of these different cultures transformed Egypt into the multicultural society that it would become in the next few centuries. Despite some of the tensions between these groups, over time, the Late Period kings were able to uphold the cultural traditions of ancient Egypt. Older texts and artworks were maintained and preserved; many of them were rewritten and copied for this purpose. The worship of many of the Old Kingdom mortuary cults was revived in old centers such as Thebes, something that further contributed to upholding the long tradition of ancient Egyptian heritage.

The internal problems of the failing Assyrian Empire were exploited in the later decades of the 7th century BCE. Egypt was able to briefly take over Palestine once Assyrian authority crumbled, but it only retained it until around 605 BCE, when King Nebuchadnezzar of the rising Neo-Babylonian Empire defeated the Egyptians at the Battle of Carchemish. King Necho II (c. 610–595 BCE), despite his defeat against the Babylonians, was able to contribute to the development of Egyptian commerce and the navy, forging closer links with the classical Greek civilization, which had been on the rise after centuries of stagnation during the Greek Dark Ages.

The 6th century brought with it a succession of ambitious kings, all descendants of Psamtik I, who unsuccessfully tried to challenge the rising dominance of the Neo-Babylonian Empire in the Near East. Necho II was succeeded by Psamtik II (c. 595–589 BCE), whose main achievement was a campaign to the south to finally put an end to the Kushites, who still had designs on Upper Egypt.

King Apries (c. 589–570 BCE) launched an offensive into the Levant, but he was unable to force the Babylonians out of the region. King Nebuchadnezzar was able to take Jerusalem, force the local Jewish people into exile to Babylon, and destroy the Temple of Solomon in 586 BCE. The fall of Jerusalem also marked the migration of thousands of Jews into the Egyptian territories. Many of them subsequently joined the army.

In the aftermath, King Apries organized a military expedition into the Greek colony of Cyrenaica in modern-day Libya, some six hundred miles west of the Nile Delta. The long and tenuous campaign caused great instability in the Egyptian army and led to an insurrection back home by Amasis or Ahmose II. This man was able to successfully depose Apries in 570 BCE. As the last great king of the Twenty-sixth Dynasty, Amasis decided to adopt a defensive foreign policy and work on domestic development to better revive the struggling Egyptian state.

Although his efforts managed to revitalize the Egyptian-Greek relations that had been strained by the attack on Cyrene, Egypt lagged behind the emerging regional powers of western Asia. The rising Persian Empire was able to enter Babylon in October 539 BCE, having already consolidated its power in modern-day Iran, thanks to the efforts of King Cyrus the Great, before moving on to the Phoenician cities of the Levant.

Cyrus's successor, Cambyses II (530–522 BCE), took the fight to Egypt in 526 BCE. By this time, Amasis had passed away and had been succeeded by his son, Psamtik III, who was only king for a few months before his defeat against the Persian forces under Cambyses. The Persian king was able to take over the Egyptian lands, reaching as far south as Napata and turning Egypt into a Persian satrapy. For the first time in history, Egypt had been fully conquered by a completely foreign empire. Despite this, the final few centuries of ancient Egyptian history were still full of important developments, which resulted in a unique transformation of the Egyptian social and cultural spheres and, ultimately, the adoption of a new identity for the civilization.

Chapter Five – Persian, Greek, and Roman Egypt

In this chapter, we will take a look at ancient Egypt during the final few centuries of its existence. After the conquest by Achaemenid Persia, Egypt became a satrapy, an administrative unit ruled by those appointed by the Persian rulers. During this time, the Achaemenid emperors would be considered pharaohs. In the 4th century BCE, Alexander the Great defeated the Achaemenids and took over Egypt himself, leading to its Hellenization, introducing Greek culture and synthesizing it with aspects of local cultures. Alexander also founded the city of Alexandria, which would become the future Egyptian capital and one of the most important cities in the world. We will also take a look at the political and cultural developments in Egypt under Alexander's successors, the Ptolemaic dynasty, which ended with the Roman conquest of Egypt in the 1st century BCE.

From the Achaemenids to Alexander

The Achaemenid conquest was unlike anything ever experienced throughout the history of ancient Egypt up until that point. At that time, the Persian Empire was the largest and the most powerful political entity in the world, stretching from Anatolia to the Indus River and including an array of different peoples, nations, cultures, and polities within it. The Persians had long-standing traditions of their own and a distinct culture, though they were far more tolerant than some of the later conquerors who would try their hand at controlling Egypt.

We can say in hindsight that Persian rulers were aware of the history and former might of ancient Egypt. They acknowledged the importance of controlling Egypt, something that added to their already exalted status as "kings of kings." This period in Egyptian history was marked by everchanging power dynamics between the Egyptians and Persian rulers.

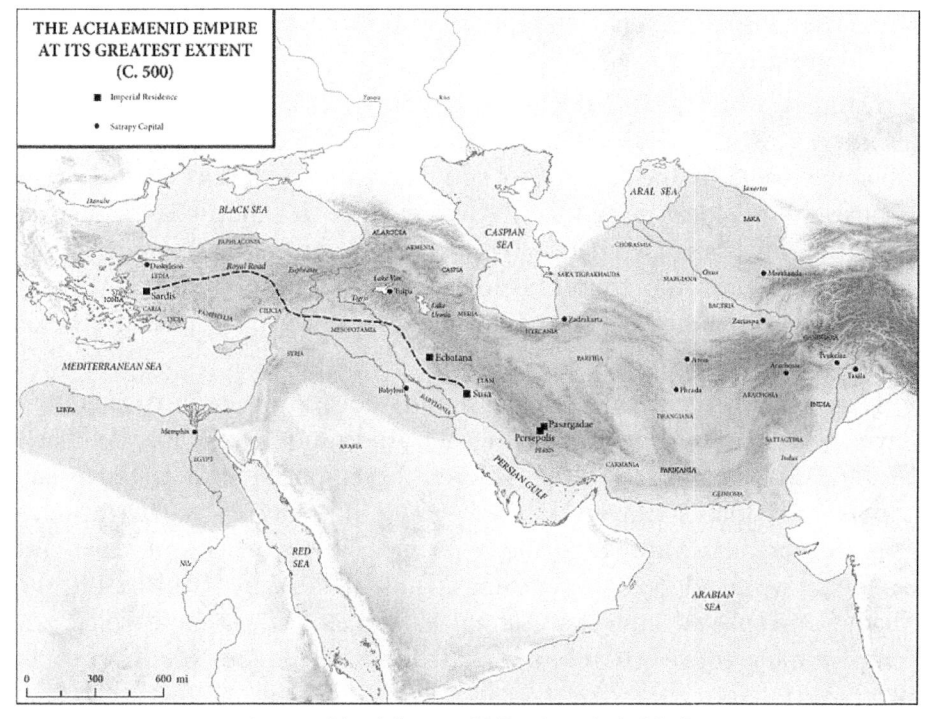

A map of the Achaemenid Empire at its height.[12]

Cambyses II was recognized as the next pharaoh and is considered to be the founder of the Twenty-seventh Dynasty of ancient Egypt, which only includes his descendants. None of them actually ruled from Egypt. Instead, this task was delegated to local or foreign bureaucrats, whose responsibility was to extract taxes from Egyptian lands and send them over to the base of the Persian Empire in modern-day Iran.

Persian rulers had to accept the special notion of kingship that had been present in Egypt for centuries. By declaring themselves as the continuers of the ancient tradition of pharaohs, they legitimized themselves as the rightful rulers of the Egyptian people. They adopted the full royal titles and represented themselves in the Egyptian tradition.

Still, pushing this image was difficult at first. The only known action of Cambyses II during his brief stay in Egypt was to defund many of the temples. In the Persian ruler's eyes, the religious class held a lot of sway and power in Egypt, and the decision to reduce the income that flowed into their pockets was necessary for better control. This resulted in widespread anti-Cambyses propaganda, which is attested to by Herodotus, who mentions his ruthless methods of ruling Egypt. In reality, Cambyses respected local Egyptian traditions and never undermined their importance.

Darius I, who succeeded Cambyses II in 522 BCE, was different from his predecessor, as he partially reversed his policies. He gave more influence back to the priests to win back their support and donated extensively to local temples. Egypt, as well as the western Libyan territories, including Cyrenaica, were reorganized into one Persian satrapy, with its center in Memphis. The administrators of the satrapies—satraps—then installed regional governors throughout the Egyptian lands for better administration.

Darius I also managed to defeat the first local uprising in Achaemenid Egypt, which was led by a man who declared himself Pharaoh Petubastis III. The Achaemenid king also ordered the codification of Egyptian laws into text so that a universal codex could be referred to during legal disputes, greatly improving the existing system in Egypt. He also personally visited Egypt several times, most notably in 497 BCE, during which he replaced the first satrap Aryandes with a new ruler and completed the construction of a canal that connected the Nile River to the Red Sea.

Such interest in local affairs gained Darius the Great much respect from the Egyptian people. Darius himself greatly respected the skills and traditions of the Egyptians. He used many local artisans for his extensive building projects in Persia and included Egypt in the increasingly cosmopolitan empire, which reached its greatest extent under the king.

Xerxes I ascended the Persian throne in 486 BCE and became the next pharaoh of the Twenty-seventh Dynasty, though he never actually visited Egypt. Unlike Darius, Xerxes's policy regarding Egypt was far less tolerant. He instantly suppressed the rebellion that broke out after his succession and installed his brother, Achaemenes, as the new satrap. Egypt had to pay Persia more tribute. Xerxes also promoted Persian beliefs at the expense of undermining local Egyptian cults.

His death in 465 BCE sparked another local uprising in Egypt by a Libyan claimant, Inaros, who managed to kill Achaemenes in battle and conquered Memphis. This was only possible because Persia had been plunged into a succession struggle after the passing of Xerxes, only to be completed with the accession of King Artaxerxes I to the throne. After consolidating his rule over the empire's lands, Artaxerxes ordered his generals to reconquer Egypt, and they obliged. Inaros was subsequently captured and crucified for instigating a rebellion, leading to the reestablishment of Persian rule for another fifty years.

The first period of Achaemenid rule ended after the death of King Darius II in 404 BCE, which led to another rebellion in Egypt. This time, the rebels were successful in expelling the Persians, albeit briefly. Amyrtaeus was able to exploit the instability in the realm created by the Persians' defeat by the Greeks and the passing of Darius II.

Amyrtaeus took control of Memphis. He is now considered to be the sole ruler of the Twenty-eighth Dynasty of ancient Egypt, ruling until around 398 BCE. This era saw increasing chaos in Egyptian politics, characterized by the quick succession of regional rulers who claimed kingship for themselves. Not a lot of documents from this period survive that could provide for a detailed understanding of the succession of events that transpired, so not much is known about the rule of Amyrtaeus and his successors.

Despite some evidence of Amyrtaeus's rule being recognized in Upper Egypt, it is reasonable to assume that he only effectively controlled the northern part of the country. He might have established relations with the Greek city of Sparta, an enemy of the Persians who were supplied by Egypt with grain in exchange for military support. Whatever the case, Amyrtaeus was overthrown by Nepherites I, who came from the city of Mendes, in 398 BCE. Nepherites I managed to defeat Amyrtaeus in an open battle. He founded the Twenty-ninth Dynasty, which would rule Egypt for about the next eighteen or so years. This dynasty continued anti-Persian policies, including further contact with the Greeks, who greatly resisted the advances of the empire during the 4th century BCE. Egypt employed more Greek mercenaries in its armies, paying them with foreign coins; Egypt had not developed a system of coinage by this time. King Hakor or Achoris (c. 393–380 BCE) managed to rebuild some of the traditional Egyptian temples and monuments during his reign, including the temple of Amun at Karnak. Ever since the Achaemenid conquest, building activities undertaken in Egypt had been extremely limited. Though no extensive records of it survive, there is evidence that Persian forces tasked with reconquering Egypt were defeated by Achoris in the later years of his reign, most likely between 385 and 382 BCE.

King Achoris was succeeded by his general, Nekhtnebef or Nectanebo I, who usurped the throne after the death of the king in 380 BCE. Nectanebo founded the Thirtieth Dynasty, which ruled for the next four decades or so. During this period, Egypt was relatively safe from Persian advances, as the once-great foreign empire was still experiencing domestic problems and had been unable to restore its former might. The Egyptians were able to defeat another Persian force around 373 BCE, thanks to disagreements within the Persian high command. This led to Persia briefly abandoning its designs to reconquer Egypt, leading to decades of relative stability.

As the third and final ruler of the Thirtieth Dynasty, Nectanebo II ascended the throne around 359 BCE and was also the last native king who ruled ancient Egypt. By the time of his reign, the presence of foreign mercenaries in the Egyptian army had already taken a toll on the economy, with the pharaoh being unable to reverse the gradual decline Egypt was experiencing.

The revitalized Persian Empire, under Artaxerxes III, organized two expeditions into Egypt. The first one, in 350 BCE, was repelled, but the Persians returned seven years later with a larger force, leading to the reconquest of Egypt. King Nectanebo II was forced to flee to Nubia, and Artaxerxes III was recognized as the new pharaoh.

The second Achaemenid conquest of Egypt lasted until the year 332 BCE. Achaemenid rulers were not tolerant like Darius I and Cambyses II had been, leading to their unpopularity throughout Egypt. The brief restoration of Achaemenid rule over Egypt is referred to as the Thirty-first Dynasty. It experienced internal instability, including a rebellion in Nubia that nearly succeeded in overthrowing the Persian yoke. The final Persian king to rule over Egypt was Darius III, who came to the throne in 336 BCE.

Alexander's Conquest and the Ptolemaic Dynasty

In 332 BCE, several years into his offensive against the Persian Empire, Macedon's Alexander the Great conquered Egypt. By this time, Alexander had slowly pushed the Persians out of their westernmost territories, defeating them on multiple occasions in Thrace, Anatolia, and the Levant. This considerably weakened the Persian Empire, which moved its forces beyond Mesopotamia to await the inevitable Macedonian offensive. At the beginning of the year, Alexander's army took Tyre and then Gaza before turning its attention to Egypt—one of the richest provinces still under the control of the Persian Empire.

However, the Egyptians, instead of putting up a resistance against the foreign conqueror, viewed him as a liberator from the tenuous rule of the Persians. Alexander was welcomed into Egypt without fighting a battle. He proceeded to journey to the western Siwa Oasis, located in the desert. Alexander wanted to meet with the Oracle of Amun, who, according to mythology, dwelled in the oasis. Supposedly, the oracle confirmed Alexander's right to the throne of Egypt and even asserted his divine ancestry as the successor to Amun himself. This helped the Macedonian ruler legitimize his rule over Egypt, which most likely officially began in Memphis with his coronation in the same year.

Afterward, Alexander decided to found a city that bore his name on the Mediterranean coast. He began work on the magnificent city of Alexandria, which would be designed by Dinocrates of Rhodos, an experienced architect who laid the foundations of a grid plan that would be followed by subsequent builders. About three centuries after its founding, Alexandria became a bustling metropolis with around half a million inhabitants.

Alexander the Great soon left Egypt to complete his conquest of the Persian Empire before his unexpected death in 323 BCE. Upon leaving, he delegated the control of Egypt, including that of the western Libyan territories of Cyrenaica, to Cleomenes of Naucratis. Naucratis was a small Greek trading colony in Egypt located in the Nile Delta. Cleomenes ruled Egypt as a satrap, retaining the Persian title and even having correspondence with Alexander before the latter's death in Babylon.

According to tradition, the title of the pharaoh of Egypt should have passed to Alexander's successor in 323 BCE, but this was impossible because of the crisis that broke out after his death. Without a strong and influential relative of Alexander to take over control of the vast empire, the territories conquered by Alexander would be divided by his generals following years of struggle known as the Wars of the Diadochi.

Several major polities would eventually emerge after the death of Alexander, including the Seleucid Empire under General Seleucus, which came to control the majority of the territories formerly under the Macedonian Empire. Ptolemy, one of Alexander's closest Macedonian allies, inherited Egypt and Cyrenaica, at first nominally ruling as a satrap. Ptolemy retrieved Alexander's body from Babylon and transported it all the way to Memphis before burying Alexander in a specially made tomb in Alexandria. Ptolemy also managed to defend Egypt from the military advances of his rival generals, defeating Perdiccas, who had taken over as regent after Alexander's death and wished to keep the empire intact, in 321 BCE.

After Perdiccas's failed invasion, Ptolemy exercised his rulership over Egypt as a satrap until 305 BCE, when he officially declared himself the rightful king of Egypt and the continuer of the long tradition of divinely blessed pharaohs, assuming the full royal titles and founding the Ptolemaic dynasty. The Greek dynasty ruled Egypt for almost the next three hundred years.

Ptolemaic Egypt was a special period in the history of ancient Egypt. This era is also dubbed the Hellenistic period, which gains its name from the ancient name for Greece, Hellas. As the name suggests, the Hellenistic period resulted in the spread of Greek culture and way of life throughout the former conquests of Alexander, reaching as far as the Indus River in the region known as Bactria. Alexander's generals were Greeks, and the kingdoms they established after his death, much like Ptolemy had done in Egypt, were modeled after the systems in ancient Greece.

It is difficult to fully emphasize the cultural and material impact this period left behind in the Mediterranean and Near East. New cities, like Alexandria in Egypt or Antioch in Syria, were modeled after the biggest cities in ancient Greece. They had their own agoras, theaters, gymnasiums, and circuses, which were sometimes exact replicas of similar buildings found in ancient Greek city-states. Greek mythology and system of beliefs often merged with local belief systems, resulting in the development of unique religions and cults that bore great resemblance to each other. The Greek language became a lingua franca of the ancient world.

Trade flourished between these distant regions, resulting in more economic growth and prosperity, though wars between Alexander's successor states were common. Major urban centers became places for learning and philosophical debates, leading to the creation of new literary works that became a staple of the ancient Greek civilization. Much material evidence from this age that points directly to ancient Greek influences survives. Such evidence has been discovered in Egypt, Anatolia, modern-day Iran, and Afghanistan.

Arguably, these changes were manifested most profoundly in Ptolemaic Egypt, where an already four-thousand-year-old civilization was Hellenized in a unique way. General Ptolemy himself, who would later become known as Soter or "savior," seemed to have understood the importance of local Egyptian beliefs, including the notion of Egyptian kingship. Even before his adoption of the title of pharaoh and basileus (a Greek title that means "monarch" and would eventually be used by Roman emperors), he envisioned himself as the restorer of the traditional Egyptian kingship, which had been disrupted during Persian rule. This can be attested to by his stela, which emphasizes his intentions and pays respects to local Egyptian deities like Horus. For about the next century and a half, Ptolemaic Egypt emerged as the most dominant and culturally advanced successor kingdom to Alexander's empire. Ptolemy I would rule until 282 BCE. He spent most of his time participating in military campaigns against his Greek rivals.

Under his successor, Ptolemy II Philadelphus, many sociocultural, economic, and administrative shifts would be undertaken in Egypt. Though the Greek civilization was not as old as Egypt, it was far more advanced in certain respects, including when it came to the bureaucracy and state administration. In 285 BCE, after Ptolemy II had been made a co-ruler alongside his father, a general census was undertaken, which measured Egypt's population and resources. This would be just one of the measures that eventually contributed to the massive economic growth experienced by Egypt during the first century and a half of the Ptolemaic dynasty. The Greek method of governance, which relied on a carefully crafted administrative system to cater to individual region's needs, led to greater agricultural yields. Under the Ptolemies, several new agricultural practices and crops were introduced to the fertile Nile River Valley. Though the realm's lands were still technically under the ownership of the king, a new class of landed aristocracy soon emerged, which was able to cultivate and look after its own lands.

It is important to understand that the Ptolemies often reinforced their own image as the Greek-Macedonian rulers of Egypt, even though their depictions featured traditional pharaonic characteristics and titles. In addition to the establishment of a complex bureaucratic system where the responsibilities of different government administrators were often intertwined to allow for more efficient regional rule, the city of Alexandria symbolized the Greekness of Egypt under the Ptolemies. Initially, the importance of Alexandria stemmed from the fact that it had been founded by Alexander the Great, who was revered by the Ptolemies as both a great ruler and warrior. As the city began to grow and adopt its distinctly Greek look, it also obtained political and economic importance.

Ptolemy I transferred the royal court to the new city from Memphis, marking the beginning of a new era for Egyptian politics. Its strategic position resulted in Alexandria becoming a trading hub with the largest port in all of the Mediterranean and one of the Seven Wonders of the Ancient World—the Lighthouse of Alexandria –which stood at over one hundred meters tall and was constructed under Ptolemy II. The monumental scale of the lighthouse reflected a return back to the prosperous times of Egypt. Soon enough, Alexandria was a dynamic metropolis, a place where people from all backgrounds traveled in order to exchange their goods and thoughts.

Ptolemy I Soter.[13]

The Ptolemies were behind the city's development into an intellectual hub, inviting artists, scientists, and philosophers from all over the Hellenistic world into their court. The crowning jewel that reflected the cultural achievement of Alexandria was its Great Library, established under Ptolemy I, which housed the largest collection of books. Scholars translated texts into different languages, generating and preserving knowledge on a previously unseen scale. Many of the world's most important thinkers operated from Alexandria under the patronage of the Ptolemies, including Euclid, the "Father of Geometry"—whose works were instrumental in the development of the field of mathematics. Scientists like Archimedes and Eratosthenes, who contributed to our understanding of the natural world, both of them Hellenes, also benefited from the repository of knowledge that was the city of Alexandria. Alexandria's importance as an economic, political, and cultural hub would last for about a thousand years after its founding by Alexander the Great, and much of its development was because of the Ptolemies.

Ptolemaic rule over Egypt was characterized by an increasing number of distinctive features. All of the male rulers of the dynasty took the name Ptolemy and adopted the Egyptian practice of marrying their own sisters and ruling jointly with their wives. Female members of the dynasty mostly took the name Cleopatra, Berenice, or Arsinoe. This practice made the Ptolemaic rulership unique in a way, though it led to many complications when it came to dynastic or marriage relations inside the royal house. There were also severe health complications that sprang up after generations of inbreeding and incestuous relations. Many rulers of the Ptolemaic dynasty, both male and female, suffered from health problems, such as obesity and weak immune systems, which put a strain on their well-being. Ptolemy II was the first one to marry his sister, Arsinoe, and the latter assumed so much importance that she was depicted on coins and deified after her death.

The deification of the Ptolemaic rulers was a common phenomenon. The Ptolemies did not suppress the local Egyptian religion; instead, they adopted it and built temples and shrines dedicated to different Egyptian deities. During the Ptolemaic period, many of the old temples were rebuilt, restored, or maintained, something that resulted in the depictions of Ptolemaic rulers in many temples. The Ptolemies also tried to equalize local Egyptian deities with similar gods from the Greek pantheon. As such, Amun was identified with Zeus, with both deities occupying a central role in the two cultures. This was perhaps the most evident example of

Egypt's Hellenization under the Ptolemies.

The administration they set up clearly favored the Greek elite over the Egyptian majority. Greeks and Egyptians had separate courts, were in separate units inside the kingdom's military, and could occupy different governmental offices. The Greeks enjoyed great privileges, while the native Egyptians had to increasingly Hellenize if they wanted to rise to positions of power.

The Rise and Fall of Ptolemaic Egypt

The Ptolemaic dynasty exercised its rule over Egypt for about the next three centuries. The first few decades after the dynasty's establishment saw extensive warfare against Ptolemy I's rivals. The general-turned-pharaoh wanted to gain control of as much of Alexander's conquests as possible, leading to conflicts over the control of Palestine and Cyprus. He even managed to occupy the Greek city of Corinth for a brief period in addition to other possessions in the Aegean, which contributed to the establishment of Egypt as a Mediterranean power. However, this did not prevent Ptolemaic Egypt from being involved in countless wars after Ptolemy I's death. During the 3rd century BCE, the Ptolemies went to war five times with the Seleucids alone, mostly contesting their possessions in the Levant.

The most successful of these campaigns were undertaken by Ptolemy III Euergetes (246-221 BCE) after his sister, who had been married off to the Seleucid royal dynasty to facilitate peace between the two powers, was murdered. His forces decisively defeated King Seleucus II, reaching as far as Babylon while establishing firmer control over the sea.

In hindsight, it was under Ptolemy III that Ptolemaic Egypt reached the zenith of its power. Its navy essentially controlled most of the eastern Mediterranean coast, and the king's possessions in Syria resulted in the influx of global trade into Egyptian lands. In addition to his military victories, Ptolemy III extensively contributed to the development of the repository at the Great Library of Alexandria and restored the Temple of Horus at Edfu, one of the best-preserved examples of ancient Egyptian architecture to this day.

His successor, Ptolemy IV Philopator, ascended the throne in 221 BCE and ruled for the next sixteen years. Unlike his predecessor, Ptolemy IV did not possess a strong personality and was subsequently under the influence of his courtiers. In 217, he was able to achieve a crucial victory against the Seleucids at the Battle of Raphia, where the combined number of soldiers reached about 150,000. This victory cemented control of Syria and the Levant into Ptolemaic hands for nearly the next two decades. His reign marked the beginning of a series of local Egyptian outbreaks in the southern part of the kingdom, which would continue in a systematic fashion until well into the 2nd century BCE. The problems that arose in Upper Egypt during this period became more prominent under the reign of Ptolemy V Epiphanes (205-180 BCE). They were mostly caused by the systematic discriminatory treatment of Egyptians by their Greek rulers, although other factors, such as the defeat of the Egyptian army by the Seleucids at the Battle of Panium in 198 BCE, contributed to rising instability. Though the Ptolemies were able to reestablish their control over the southern part of the kingdom, revolts and secession attempts would plague the rest of their time as kings of Egypt.

The accession of Ptolemy V to the throne led to the creation of what is arguably the most important archaeological discovery that relates to ancient Egypt—the Rosetta Stone. The stela contains a royal decree about the activities of the new king toward Egyptian temples and shrines throughout the realm. It also mentions the rebellion that took place in Upper Egypt and highlights the fact that the king was able to restore his rule after years of instability. Aside from its importance as a royal decree and a source that allows us to better understand the political dynamics in Ptolemaic Egypt during the reign of Ptolemy V, the significance of the Rosetta Stone lies in the fact that it contains the decree in three scripts: Koine Greek, Egyptian Demotic, and Egyptian hieroglyphs. Discovered in the very late 18th century during the Napoleonic campaigns into Egypt, the Rosetta Stone enabled us to decipher the ancient Egyptian hieroglyphic script and better understand ancient Egyptian history. Currently, the stone is on public display at the British Museum.

Ptolemy V's reign marked the beginning of the Ptolemaic dynasty's decline, which became increasingly engulfed in dynastic struggles after the accession of the pharaoh, who was only twelve years old when he was officially crowned king. The defeat at Panium greatly complicated the existing political situation, leading to the loss of Egypt's possessions in the Levant. The Ptolemies also had to cater to the interests of the new rising power in the Mediterranean, the Roman Republic, which was slowly expanding eastward after achieving a decisive victory against Carthage in the Second Punic War (218—201 BCE). The Romans moved against the Seleucids in 192 BCE, and Ptolemy V unsuccessfully tried to gain Roman favor despite offering them military and financial support in the war. For the next decade, Ptolemy V planned the invasion of Seleucid Syria to exact revenge for the defeat suffered during the previous war, but he died unexpectedly in 180 BCE. He was perhaps poisoned by his courtiers who were unsupportive of his foreign policies.

Ptolemy VI, who was still an infant, succeeded his father the same year, with his mother, Cleopatra I, acting as regent before her death in 176 BCE. Six years later, Seleucid King Antiochus IV invaded Egypt and successfully defeated the Egyptian forces. In fact, he managed to essentially reduce Egypt into a protectorate, installing the young Ptolemy VI as a puppet king at Memphis and his brother, Ptolemy VII, as a ruler in Alexandria, leading to the fragmentation of the dynasty. Antiochus was expelled from Egypt thanks to Roman interference, though the relations between the two brothers were never normalized.

The rising influence of Rome and the dynastic struggles between the Ptolemies resulted in the ever-increasing presence of Rome in the domestic politics of Egypt. The two brothers quarreled until Ptolemy VI's death in 145 BCE, after which Ptolemy VII usurped the throne and co-ruled Egypt with his sister-wife, Cleopatra II, until 116 BCE.

The final century or so of Ptolemaic rule was chaotic, to say the least. The Roman Republic recognized the benefits of exercising its behind-the-scenes influence over Egypt, which was no longer politically or militarily strong enough to challenge it. The Romans saw Egypt as a great land to have because the fertile Nile Valley guaranteed the supply of grain into Roman lands, which made it possible for Rome to focus on expansion.

Feeble Ptolemaic rulers had to rely increasingly on Roman support after the death of their predecessor, and dynastic struggles rendered it impossible to maintain a cohesive rule. In 80 BCE, Ptolemy XII Auletes—"the flute-player"—ascended the throne and ruled until 51 BCE, though not without problems. Amidst growing insecurity and threats over his position, he briefly fled Egypt in 55 BCE, only to be restored thanks to the efforts of Roman General Pompey and his allies. In 52 BCE, Ptolemy XII Auletes designated his daughter, Cleopatra VII, and his son, Ptolemy XIII, as his successors. They would be the last of the Ptolemies to rule Egypt.

Roman Egypt

The succession of Cleopatra VII and Ptolemy XIII faced internal difficulties from the get-go, as the latter was favored by the powerful Egyptian courtiers. It is clear that the two did not have a good relationship, and it appears that both of them tried to assert their sole rule over the kingdom by issuing royal decrees that omitted the other's name. Egypt was essentially engulfed in a civil war, though neither side was strong enough to fully take control of the political situation.

The matter was even more complicated because of another factor: Rome. By the time of their accession, the co-rulers of Egypt owed a large debt to the Roman Republic. Additionally, Rome was experiencing a civil war between Julius Caesar and Pompey. The latter had been forced out of Italy by the former, and he decided to take refuge in Egyptian lands, with the Egyptians providing some military assistance in the hopes that it would be beneficial in the long term when it came to repaying the existing debt.

However, Ptolemy XIII, influenced by his courtiers and fearing that Pompey might try to use Egypt as a future base of operations for his actions in the Roman civil war, ambushed and killed the Roman general in September 48 BCE. He sent the embalmed head of Pompey to Julius Caesar, who soon arrived in Egypt and expressed his disappointment, not only in Ptolemy's actions but also regarding the whole unstable situation in Egypt. He knew that the civil war was over, so it was in his interest to make peace between the two rulers of Egypt so that the Egyptian grain supply did not stop.

Caesar's arrival in Alexandria resulted in a series of skirmishes between the Roman and Egyptian forces. Ptolemy hoped to restore his sole rule over the city and the kingdom. Caesar favored the twenty-two-year-old Cleopatra. The Roman forces were victorious at the Battle of the Nile. King Ptolemy died, reportedly having drowned in the river. This left Cleopatra the most legitimate and the strongest claimant to the throne. By the summer of 47 BCE, she had already married another of her brothers, Ptolemy XIV, who technically became her co-ruler.

However, it was clear that the Egyptian queen had other plans for herself and the future of her realm. She embarked on a two-month-long tour of the Nile with Caesar and developed a close relationship with the Roman dictator. When he left for Rome, Cleopatra was pregnant with a son, whom she named Caesarion ("Little Caesar"). The queen and her son traveled to Rome to stay with Caesar, though they came back to Egypt immediately after his assassination in 44 BCE.

Sculpture of Cleopatra with a royal diadem.[14]

Cleopatra's associations with prominent Roman rulers did not end with Caesar. After his death, Rome was engulfed in another bloody civil war between Mark Antony and Octavian, the future emperor. The two had briefly tried to rule together as part of the Second Triumvirate, but their relations quickly deteriorated and resulted in an all-out conflict in 32 BCE. Octavian accused the third member of the Triumvirate—Lepidus—of staging a rebellion and eliminated him in 36 BCE. Mark Antony formed a power base in the eastern part of the republic.

In 41 BCE, Cleopatra visited Mark Antony at his seat in Tarsus on the southeastern Mediterranean coast of Anatolia, and the two subsequently developed a romance. The romance resulted in a marriage and three children. The relationship between the two was mutually beneficial for both. It guaranteed the military and political protection of Egypt by Mark Antony. In exchange, the Roman general took control of the valuable Egyptian grain, which would put a strain on Octavian back in Rome.

Meanwhile, the Roman Senate adopted an increasingly hostile view toward Cleopatra. They thought she wished to manipulate prominent Roman leaders and play them off each other for her own benefit. Their anger was justified. In 34 BCE, Mark Antony agreed to bequeath much of the eastern Roman territories to her four children, something that would have resulted in the loss of these rich lands.

Unfortunately, the grandiose plans to divide the eastern Roman lands and forge a new political power centered around Egypt that rivaled Rome were short-lived, as Octavian declared war on Mark Antony in 32 BCE. Favored by the elites at Rome, he launched an ambitious campaign against his rival and decisively defeated his forces at the naval Battle of Actium in September of 31 BCE. Mark Antony's fleet, reinforced by a small Egyptian force provided by Cleopatra, was defeated in the Ionian Sea off the coast of Greece. Many of his soldiers defected to the rival camp. Antony was chased to Alexandria by the remainder of Octavian's forces.

Ten months later, Octavian reached Alexandria and took the city with little resistance. Fearing their capture and expecting to be humiliated before their death, Cleopatra and Mark Antony committed suicide in August 30 BCE before enemy soldiers could get to them. Thus, the three centuries of Ptolemaic rule over Egypt came to an end. The era of Roman Egypt had started.

The main focus of Rome was to strengthen the empire and extract as many resources, taxes, slaves, and soldiers from its provinces as possible. Because the Roman Empire was so large and controlled a wide range of cultures and peoples with different levels of social and political organization, this objective was modified to fit the needs of the provinces.

Luckily for the Romans, by the time of Octavian's conquest of Egypt, it had already been a thriving millennia-long civilization with high levels of political and social development. This made it easier for Rome to integrate Egypt into its empire, though important changes were adopted to make sure that Egypt was sufficiently Romanized. Egypt was different from the other imperial provinces because it was considerably richer. Egypt's wealth did not only stem from the fertile Nile River and the food it generated for the empire. Due to its location, Egypt played a central role in Roman trade. By 100 CE, the city of Alexandria was the second-largest city in the empire after Rome, though its wealth arguably made it just as important as the Eternal City.

The main concern when it came to ruling Egypt—or Aegyptus, as it was called by the Romans—was administrative efficiency, which allowed for a more rigid control of the taxes and resources that flowed into Rome. Luckily, Roman bureaucracy was as efficient as it got for classical antiquity. The rule of the province was delegated to a prefect, who essentially acted as a viceroy and answered directly to the emperor. The office of the prefect was not hereditary, and hundreds of different officials would serve in the role until the mid-4th century, before the fall of the Western Roman Empire.

The first of the rulers was Gaius Cornelius Gallus, who only ruled for four years before falling out with the emperor. He was replaced in 26 BCE. As the most important and powerful official in Egypt, he delegated control of different districts and administrative divisions to lower figures in the hierarchy, who were tasked with collecting taxes, settling legal disputes, and raising armies when needed. However, the prefect had the final say in the most important matters, and petitions and requests to his office were frequent. Other officials had limited say in province-wide matters, but they had virtual autonomy in their administrative districts. This was the system Rome modified and adapted to the needs of different conquered territories.

Economically, Egypt's function did not change a lot under Roman rule, though the privatization of many of its lands led to the emergence of a new, rich landowner class. Adopting the old Greek model in which wealthy individuals had to finance public works and contribute extensively to the growth of local communities, the Romans were successful in boosting the development of much of Egypt's previously smaller and less important towns and villages. This was fundamental to both the Greek and Roman understanding of what it meant to be a "good" member of the community, regardless of its size. Privatization also led to the development of Roman-style mansions and estates, where many peasants and poor people were employed.

The Romans also allowed for the minting and circulation of the tetradrachm coins, which had been introduced to Egypt by the Greeks and were produced at Alexandria. Romans minted their own coins—the denarius—the value of which was eventually equal to that of the tetradrachm. This was a necessary change, as Rome began to increasingly take over the Hellenized world, where the Greek-style currency was in circulation. All of these changes resulted in a boom in Egyptian trade, both domestically within its regions and in the flow of foreign goods into the region.

Egypt also acted as a gateway for Mediterranean trade to Asia through the Red Sea and vice versa. The various taxes and customs tariffs on different goods further enriched Egyptian lands, which reached the peak of their wealth during the Pax Romana ("Roman Peace") by the end of the 2nd century CE.

The concept of Roman citizenship was at the heart of Roman society, which included millions of people from different ethnic, cultural, linguistic, and religious backgrounds. Roman citizens constituted a minority of all of Rome's inhabitants. They enjoyed a special set of privileges, such as the right to participate in the government. This continued until the early 3rd century CE when Emperor Caracalla issued an edict that declared all free men within the borders of the empire Roman citizens.

Before then, Romans tried to reorganize and clearly distinguish the different strata of Egyptian society. Roman citizens, both ethnically Latins and those who had attained citizenship through various means, stood at the top of the hierarchy. They were followed by the Greeks, who constituted an increasing number of people in Egypt since Alexander's conquest. Greek citizens in urban areas had more rights and privileges than their Egyptian counterparts, thanks to Roman favoritism. Rural Egyptians, such as peasants, constituted the lowest class in Roman Egypt.

However, social mobility was possible. For example, one could obtain citizenship by serving in the auxiliary army. Members of the higher classes had more rights, but it also meant they had more responsibilities and a higher tax burden. The Roman legal system also bestowed different punishments on people of different classes.

The Romans understood the level of influence exercised by the Greek elite, and their actions were directed toward reinforcing the existing social stratification. This was true in the cultural sphere as well, as Alexandria continued to enjoy its role as one of the most prominent intellectual centers of the Mediterranean and the Near East. The foundations laid by the Ptolemies certainly showed themselves during the Roman era. Rural areas of Egypt continued to practice traditional Egyptian belief systems, which had gained a distinct Hellenized outlook since the late 4th century BCE. The animal cults that had risen to prominence after the spread of Hellenic culture continued to enjoy their popularity. Interestingly, the cults of the Roman emperors were worshiped extensively throughout

Egypt, which was reminiscent of venerating the divine cults of the pharaohs. Technically, the Roman emperors were the continuers of the pharaonic kingship, though this was no longer as prominent after the fall of the Ptolemaic dynasty.

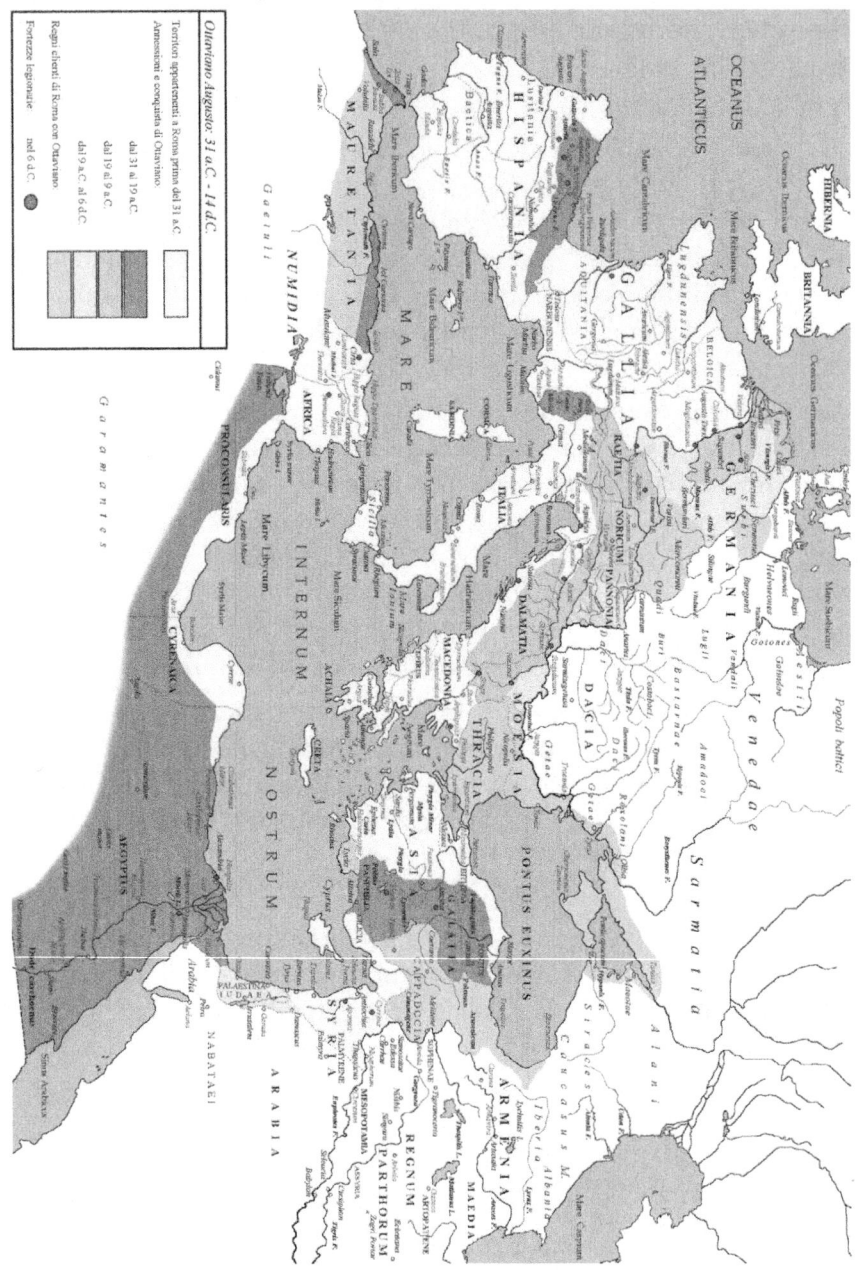

A political map of the Roman Empire with its provinces. [15]

From Augustus to the Sassanids

The Romans took pride in defending and controlling Egypt, as they were aware of the consequences that would follow the loss of the rich province. The empire maintained a relatively smaller force of up to two or three legions in Egypt, with a total number of about twelve thousand to fifteen thousand soldiers. It was easy to patrol the Egyptian territories since most important centers were located along the Nile River, and the threat of a concentrated attack from a foreign power was not imminent. The Kingdom of Meroe, a successor of Kush, attempted an invasion of Roman Egypt in the late 1st century BCE, but the Roman forces managed to push the invaders back south of the First Cataract of the Nile, where they maintained the frontier.

Moreover, the North African coast was totally under the control of the Roman Empire. The only possible place that could be hostile was the Arabian Peninsula, where no strong local kingdom had emerged. Arabian tribes were mostly concentrated in the southern part of the peninsula, and the Romans mostly had good relations with them because of mutual trade interests. Instead, internal conflicts threatened the security of the province. The Roman Empire was infamous for the countless dynastic struggles that followed disputes over succession after the death of the previous emperor. In such cases, succession would be decided by whoever had the bigger army.

Prominent Roman generals, who would venture out to distant lands on military campaigns, would often be declared emperors by their legions, who were loyal only to their commander. In fact, Emperor Vespasian emerged as the sole ruler of the empire in 69 CE following a civil war known as the Year of the Four Emperors. He was proclaimed emperor in Alexandria, as his power base had been the southeastern coast of the Mediterranean. Revolts from Egyptian prefects occurred as well, such as ones during the reigns of Emperors Marcus Aurelius and Diocletian in 175 and 297 CE, respectively.

During the Crisis of the Third Century—a period of internal chaos that nearly led to the destruction of the Roman Empire—Egypt was briefly part of the breakaway Kingdom of Palmyra. Named after the Syrian city of Palmyra, the rebels revolted at a time when Rome was facing both domestic and external threats that undermined its unity. The Kingdom of Palmyra formed in 260 and lasted until 271, eventually turning into an empire. It briefly controlled the Levant, southeastern Anatolia, and Egypt.

Emperor Aurelian eventually put an end to the imperial hopes of its self-declared Queen Zenobia. These episodes of instability highlighted the scale of the economic problems Rome could experience after a temporary or permanent loss of Egypt.

Emperor Diocletian (r. 284–305) inaugurated a range of administrative reforms during his reign that changed the large Roman Empire. The empire was to be ruled by two co-emperors and their successors, who the co-emperors designated during their lifetimes. The system became known as the tetrarchy and divided the territories of the Roman Empire into four parts. Further administrative divisions were also introduced. Former provinces were subdivided into smaller counterparts. The province of Thebais, for example, which largely included the territories of historical Upper Egypt, emerged as a separate entity. However, these smaller provinces were also reorganized into larger entities called dioceses. The old province of Aegyptus, along with Cyrenaica, was united into the Diocese of the East (Diocese of Oriens). However, in the late 4th century, the Diocese of Egypt became its own separate administrative unit. Its governor had the unique title of praefectus augustalis, and its capital was Alexandria.

Diocletian's reign was also significant for two other reasons. Firstly, during his reign, the mint at Alexandria, which had produced the tetradrachms since the Ptolemaic period, was closed down. Secondly and more importantly, Diocletian was arguably the most infamous persecutor of Christians in the Roman Empire. Christianity, which originated in the Levant, had slowly spread to neighboring regions, including Egypt, where, according to Christian tradition, Saint Mark founded the Church of Alexandria.

At first, just like any other religious movement, Christianity was not a profound force. Christians were widely disfavored throughout the empire's lands, and they largely kept their faith in secret and met in small groups. They held modest congregations wherever they could, and there was not much evidence about their activities in Egypt until the 4th century when the practice of Christianity was legalized. It was later made the official religion of the Roman Empire.

By then, Alexandria had a substantial Christian population, which included prominent theologians like Clement of Alexandria and his disciple, Origen. It is important to understand that as the religion spread to different parts of the empire, it also developed. There were frequent debates and talks that tried to interpret the Gospels. The Edict of Milan, issued by Emperor Constantine the Great in 313, ended the persecution of Christians, marking a turning point for the religion and the beginning of its rapid advance throughout the empire's territories. This was followed by a gradual decline of Roman paganism. Properties that had been confiscated from Christians were returned by Roman authorities. Disputes within the church became more common.

In 325, the First Council of Nicaea met in the Greek city of Nicaea. Christian bishops from all over the world attended the meeting and debated Christian theology, issuing the Nicene Creed. The Nicene Creed pointed out the central aspects of the religion that were to be upheld by all Christians around the world. This was an effort to unite the church under one dogma, and it was largely successful, though diverging interpretations had been prevalent before and continued to emerge afterward.

Interestingly, it was the city of Alexandria where the first major schism of Christianity took place. An Alexandrian presbyter by the name of Arius postulated that Jesus, as the Son of God, was not one or equal with God the Father and was subordinate to him. The views of Arius were later advanced by his disciples, such as Aetius, and came to be called Arianism. The Arian controversy was very divisive among early Christians, leading to different religious-themed riots and rebellions against its main opponents, orthodox Christians, who rejected it at the Council of Nicaea. Arians would be a thorn in the side of Athanasius, who was appointed as the archbishop of Alexandria in 326 and served as the head of the church for almost the next half-century.

Christianity developed in a unique way in Egypt with the advent of the Coptic Orthodox Church, which was formed during the theological conflicts of the 4th and 5th centuries. The native Egyptian population of the Roman province had largely been Hellenized by that point, and the native ancient Egyptian language had adopted a new Greek-style alphabet, evolving from its hieroglyphic, hieratic, and Demotic roots. This became known as the Coptic script, the name of which derives from the Arabic name given to the people after the Muslim conquest in the 7th century, *Qibt*, a term used to describe the minority.

A separate Christian identity of the native Egyptians developed after the Council of Chalcedon, which rejected the Monophysite belief in 451. Monophysites asserted that Christ had only a divine and not a human nature. The council ruled that Christ was both fully divine and fully human through incarnation. Most Christians adopted the Chalcedonian ruling.

Egypt witnessed the development of the Miaphysite doctrine, which asserted that both divinity and humanity were united without alteration or separation into oneness in the one person of Jesus Christ. Though the Miaphysites claimed that their views were not too different from the Chalcedonian view, which became orthodox Christian doctrine in 451, their position was also ruled to be incorrect by the council. The Egyptian Miaphysite believers reorganized themselves into the Coptic Orthodox Church of Alexandria, which followed the teachings of Saint Cyril of Alexandria and split from the mainstream churches in Rome and Constantinople. This break marked a turning point and was rejected as heresy. The Coptic Orthodox Church, which moved its seat from Alexandria to Cairo following the Arab conquest of Egypt, developed a separate Egyptian identity from the rest of the Christian world. Even today, it is the largest Christian minority in all of Egypt.

Aside from the emergence of Arianism and Coptic Christianity, Egypt was one of the first centers of Christian monasticism. Many Egyptians followed in the footsteps of Saint Anthony of Egypt, a 3rd-century monk who secluded himself from society after relocating to the desert and pursuing an ascetic lifestyle reminiscent of the Christian monastic movement. The first adherents of Christian monasticism were called hermits, a name that derives from the Greek word *eremos*, which means desert. Thousands of people left Egyptian towns and villages and traveled to the desert to live completely alone, not unlike the monastic communities that developed in the medieval era. In fact, another 4th-century Egyptian monk, Saint Pachomius, was the first one to organize monastic communities in the desert. These were small village-like complexes where monastics devoted their life to regular worship and work. All of these traditions, which would later become staples of the Christian faith, trace their roots back to Egypt.

Politically, Egypt's role in the Roman Empire was transformed by the advent of Christianity. Alexandria's status as the second-most important city in the Roman Empire after Rome itself was challenged after the founding of Constantinople by Emperor Constantine the Great in May of 330. Located at the Strait of Bosphorus and designated as the new capital of the Roman Empire, which was divided into Eastern and Western counterparts, Constantinople eclipsed not only Alexandria but also Rome. Crucially, the division of the empire placed Egypt in the East, meaning that the Eastern Roman Empire benefited from Egyptian grain than the West.

The inhabitants of the Eastern Roman Empire, later to be known as the Byzantine Empire because Constantinople had been built on the older Greek town of Byzantium, considered themselves Roman. They were the continuers of the long history that had begun with the founding of Rome in 753 BCE. Of course, the Eastern Roman Empire eventually became culturally distinct from the Western Roman Empire because of the prominence of Hellenism in its territories. The fact that Egypt had been put under the jurisdiction of the Byzantines contributed to the decline of the Western Roman Empire, which eventually collapsed in 476 CE due to a wide range of factors, including instability caused by the migration of Germanic tribes into its territories in the 4th century.

The importance of Alexandria increased with the advent of Christianity. The Alexandrian Holy See was formally recognized as a leading institution during Emperor Justinian's reign in the 6th century. Justinian reorganized the Christian Church into the Pentarchy with five leading episcopal sees in Constantinople, Rome, Jerusalem, Antioch, and Alexandria. The heads of these churches, called patriarchs, gained more power and influence. Politically, Justinian wished to restore the former glory of the once-great Roman Empire, launching military campaigns to reclaim the lost lands in Europe that had fallen to the Germanic barbarians.

In light of the growing instability, the patriarch of Alexandria emerged as a leading figure in the Christian world, influencing religious and civil affairs in Egypt. The patriarchs of Alexandria were under constant pressure from the emperors in Constantinople, who recognized the importance of keeping the economically important Egypt under their firm rule. The fact that it lay at the edge of the empire made Egypt a prime target for domestic usurpers and foreign powers.

In the 7th century, the Sassanid Persian Empire, the main foreign rival of the Byzantines, invaded Egypt in 618 and eventually conquered it by 621. Though the Sassanid Persians would only rule Egypt for the next decade, the loss of the province was a massive blow to the hopes of the Byzantine Empire. Interestingly, the Sassanids recognized the existing rivalry between the adherents of the Byzantine Church in Egypt and the local Coptic Orthodox Church and favored the latter. They believed that further division would be beneficial in crushing Byzantine influence over the region and did not try to impose their own Zoroastrian religion on the inhabitants of Egypt. During this period, many of the Byzantine Orthodox churches were taken over by the Copts, leading to it being cemented as the major branch of Christianity in Egypt. The Sassanids eventually withdrew from Egypt in 628 following a peace treaty with the Byzantines, though the return of Roman rule over Egypt would only last for the next ten years.

Chapter Six – Medieval Egypt

The Muslim Conquest

Just as the Sassanids were pushing the Byzantines out of the Levant and Egypt, important developments were taking place in the Arabian Peninsula, which had largely been left unexplored and unconquered by major powers. A new religion that followed the teachings of Prophet Muhammad, Islam, was born in Arabia. The adherents of the new religion were able to slowly unite the largely nomadic peoples living in the peninsula who had never before been part of a coherent political structure, unlike their Persian or Egyptian neighbors. Muhammad led many of the military campaigns, which were justified as holy wars to spread the word and teachings of Allah, the one god of Islam. The leaders of the Rashidun Caliphate, a Muslim empire led by their caliph Abu Bakr, further expanded throughout the peninsula and even waged wars against both the Byzantines and the Sassanids.

The Arab armies quickly became known for their zeal and military prowess despite the fact that both the Byzantines and the Sassanids were much more powerful and experienced on paper. However, the Rashidun caliphs were able to exploit the unstable political situation in the region, as both great powers had been weakened after centuries of non-stop wars against each other, leaving them exposed to a concentrated offensive by another power. The Arabs decisively defeated the Byzantines at the Battle of the Yarmuk in 636 and followed it up with another important victory against the Persians at al-Qadisiyyah. Crucially, Caliph Umar was able to lay siege and take Jerusalem in 638, completing the conquest of Byzantine-held Syria and Palestine.

Having detached the rich province of Egypt from the rest of the empire, the conquest of Egypt was only a matter of time. Led by Amr ibn al-Āṣ, a general who had supposedly visited Alexandria during his youth, the four-thousand-strong detachment from the main army invaded Egypt in 639. The Arab armies took the important city of Pelusium before making their way into the central delta region, laying siege to the fortress of Babylon in May 640, where they received reinforcements that played a decisive factor in their victory. At the Battle of Heliopolis, the Arabs proceeded to defeat an army of about twenty thousand men, and it was clear that Alexandria would be the next to fall. Many Byzantine forces, disconnected from their leadership and the center of the empire (now in Anatolia), were forced to flee on ships. By 642, Alexandria had fallen to the Arabs. The city was defended by its new owners after an attempted invasion in 645 by the Byzantines to take it back. Thus began a new Islamic era in Egyptian history that would bring massive cultural and sociopolitical changes.

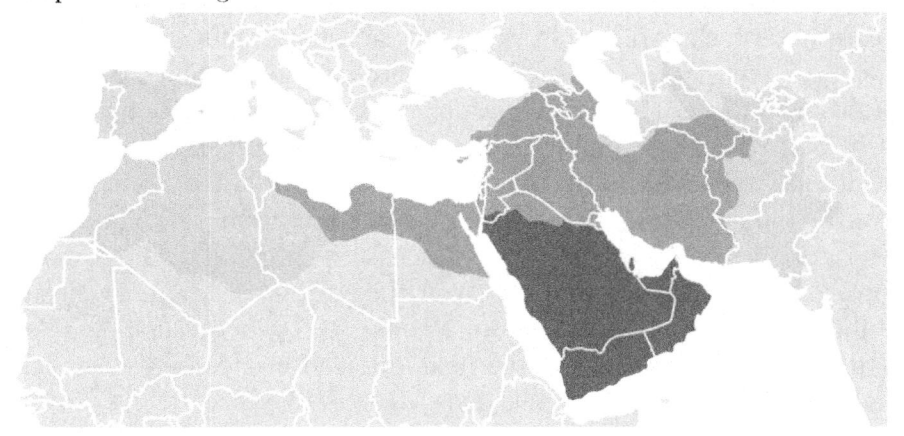

Map of the early stages of the caliphate's expansion.[16]

Unlike when Egypt was Hellenized and then Romanized centuries earlier, the Arab conquerors were more careful in reforming Egyptian society and culture early on. This was not unique to Egypt, as the Arabization of the newly conquered lands of the Levant, Iran, and the North African coast, which was added to the caliph's lands by the end of the century, was not an intense campaign. The Arabs had never before been in charge of empires, so they decided to keep the existing social and political structures largely intact to allow for a smooth transition from Byzantine rule. The Arabs did not even force their subjects to convert to

Islam despite the fact that the objective of their conquests was to spread the Islamic faith. In fact, for decades, a large portion of people who lived under Arabic rule were Christians. In Egypt, the Arabs decided to keep the Byzantine taxation system and utilized the Christian Church as an effective mechanism to collect taxes until a Muslim bureaucracy could be established.

The doctrine of Islam was central to the political structure of the Arab empires, beginning with the Rashidun Caliphate, which conquered Egypt in 642. The rulers placed a lot of emphasis on the teachings of Muhammad, as well as on the decrees and orders of the individual caliphs, who were viewed as the main defenders of the faith, not only as political leaders. For the non-Muslim inhabitants of the Arab empire, life largely went on without much disruption after the conquests were concluded. The new overlords of Egypt did not establish themselves at Alexandria, something that would have been, at first glance, the logical choice because of the importance of the city. Instead, they founded the city of al-Fusṭāṭ (Fustat) as their new capital. It was near the fortress of Babylon on the delta, which would later grow and be absorbed by the city of Cairo, which was founded in the 10th century and subsequently became the capital of Egypt. At the center of the new capital stood a mosque that bore the name of Egypt's conqueror, Amr ibn al-Āṣ, whose original encampment during the campaign had been chosen as the site to construct the city.

Because of its location, Egypt became a hub from which the Arab rulers expanded farther to the west throughout the 7th century. The port of Alexandria, which the Byzantines had built up as a center of production of their ships, was taken over by the Arabs. The new Muslim overlords of Egypt used these ships to launch multiple naval offensives against the Byzantine Greek islands of Crete and Rhodes in the 650s. Due to the successful expansion into modern-day Tunisia and Morocco under the Umayyad Caliphate, which succeeded the Rashidun Caliphate in 661, the frontiers of the Muslim conquerors kept expanding.

The only requirement from the inhabitants of Egypt was taxes. It took generations before Egypt adopted a distinctively Muslim outlook. For instance, the spoken language remained Greek, not Arabic, until at least the 8th century for the majority of Egyptians.

Still, controlling Egypt did not come without difficulties. In time, more and more Arabs emigrated and settled in the province, contributing to the

Islamization of the Egyptian lands. The role of Egypt did not really change during the transition from Byzantine to Arab rule, as the Muslim rulers regarded the province as an important economic and agricultural territory that had to supply the heart of the caliphate, which lay in Baghdad.

However, taxation sometimes faced difficulties, especially as the Arab and Muslim inhabitants of the provinces were clearly favored by the caliphate compared to their Christian counterparts, who had to pay much more. There were multiple attempted rebellions in the late 7th century, and rebellions became more frequent by the mid-8th century. Interestingly, the Coptic Egyptians showed the most resistance to the increasing tax burden, revolting in 725, 739, and 750 under Umayyad rule and in 828 and 831 under Abbasid rule. This resulted in frequent changes in leadership, as the governors appointed by the caliphs could not effectively deal with the situation. The Abbasid caliph al-Ma mun led the Arab armies that subdued the later revolts in 828, which undermined the position of the Copts and contributed to the rise in prominence of Islam.

The Tulunids, Ikhshidids, and the Fatimids

The Abbasid Caliphate was the third Islamic caliphate that was ruled by the descendants of Prophet Muhammad's uncle, Abbas ibn Abd al-Muttalib, which overthrew the Umayyad Caliphate in 750 and reached the zenith of its power around 850. The Abbasids ruled from Baghdad in Iraq, though the center of their power originated from the southeastern Caspian region, which had previously been under the control of the Persian Empire. In fact, a distinct feature of Abbasid rule was the fact that the caliphate relied heavily on Persian bureaucrats, as Persia had a far more established tradition of administration and governance than Arabia. However, this overreliance eventually resulted in the decline of the caliph's authority, which was weakened by the migration of central Asian Turkic warrior tribes in the early 10th century. The Abbasids and their predecessors, the Umayyads, had long waged wars against the Turks, having expanded into the territories of central Asia where the former had dwelt as nomads. The caliphs also recognized the effectiveness and prowess of the Turkic warriors, enslaving many of them and forcing them to serve in Arab armies. These contingents of the caliphs' armies were known as the Mamluks and were also headed by Turkic war chiefs, who would be granted pieces of land by the caliphs as payment for their services.

In the mid-9th century, the Abbasid Caliphate assigned control of Egypt to Turkic leaders instead of appointing an Arab governor, as had been the practice for the past two centuries. The main reason behind this decision was the continued uprisings that took place in Egypt, which required quick and decisive action to be subdued. In 868, Ahmad ibn Tulun, a Turk, was sent as a governor to Egypt after his adoptive father, a Turk general by the name of Babak, had delegated the position to him. Instead of more effectively ruling the important province in the name of the caliph, ibn Tulun proceeded to consolidate his own power independently from the Abbasids. He gained widespread popularity among the Egyptians after he dismissed Ibn al-Mudabbir, the administrator who had doubled the taxes on Egypt's population and had been disliked by the locals.

In time, he usurped power in the province and managed to increase his influence to the point that he could defy the Abbasid caliph in Baghdad, acting independently and breaking from the caliphate. His rise to power established the short-lived Tulunid dynasty, which would constitute an almost four-decade-long de facto independence of Egypt from the Abbasids, which contributed to the eventual decline of Abbasid authority and the rise of Egypt as an independent state.

The brief Tulunid rule over Egypt had partially been made possible because of the internal instability of the Abbasids, who were facing a slave revolt in 869, known as the Zanj Rebellion, which made it difficult to exercise rigid control over the caliphate's vast territories. Ahmad ibn Tulun was able to defeat the force sent by the caliph to reestablish his rule over Egypt and proceeded to invade the Levant himself in 878, ten years after his arrival in Egypt.

In all respects, Ahmad acted as the rightful ruler of Egypt, minting coins with his name and pursuing his own policies to strengthen his realm. To symbolize his rule over Egypt as the beginning of a new era, he founded a new capital city, Al-Qatai, near the existing capital of Fustat, where he constructed a great mosque that bore his name. Although brief, his rule over Egypt oversaw significant improvements in the region's economy, as well as interesting cultural shifts. The Mosque of Ibn Tulun, for example, was constructed in the Samarran style, adopting designs that had been prevalent in the heartland of the Abbasids in Iraq.

Ahmad ibn Tulun founded a dynasty that would independently rule Egypt for the first time since the Ptolemaic era. However, the Tulunid dynasty was not to last nearly as long as that of the Ptolemies. Ahmad's son, Khumarawayh, succeeded his father in 884 and continued to spend lavishly at the expense of the treasury his father had left behind. Feeling unthreatened by the political turmoil in the East, he even managed to strike a marriage alliance with Abbasid Caliph al-Mu'tadid's daughter in 892. The wedding cost the Tulunid ruler an arm and a leg despite the fact that the Abbasid princess brought a dowry of at least several hundred thousand dinars. The alliance was important, as the caliph essentially recognized Tulunid rule over the lands, though the Abbasids were quick to change their minds after the death of Khumarawayh in 896. Leaving a teenage son as his successor and no sufficient means to defend the realm from the caliphate, Abbasid armies managed to reconquer the lost territories and put an end to the Tulunid dynasty in 905.

However, the Abbasids were unable to restore stability in the war-torn province by appointing their own governors. In 935, this would lead to the loss of Egypt to an unruly Turkic general, Muhammad ibn Tughj, who came from the central Asian province of Sogdiana. He adopted the title ikhshīd, meaning "prince" in his native land. It would become the name of the dynasty that he established in Egypt. His actions greatly resembled that of Ahmad ibn Tulun, with the Turk general managing to defeat the Abbasid forces in Syria and maintaining a firm control over Egypt. The Ikhshidids were not apt at running such a large and developed swath of land. Their failing bureaucracy was just one of the reasons behind the dynasty's quick end in 968.

Thus, Egypt would see the establishment of a fourth dynasty in the span of just a few decades. This time, Egyptian lands were conquered and taken over by the Fatimids, who originated from North Africa and adhered to Shi'a Islam, the branch whose supporters did not recognize the caliph as the spiritual leader of the Islamic world, unlike the Abbasids. In the eyes of the Shi'a, the Abbasid caliphs were blasphemous usurpers. The Fatimids instead claimed the right to the caliphate, as they regarded themselves as the descendants of Prophet Muhammad through Fatimah, his daughter after whom the dynasty was named, and his cousin, Ali. Shi'a missionaries spread throughout the Mediterranean during the early stages of Islamic expansion in the 7th century. By the early 10th century, they had established themselves in North Africa, and in 909, they proclaimed their imam or spiritual leader, Abdullah al-Mahdi Billah, as their caliph. The Fatimids gradually expanded eastward and took over the territories of Tunis, Libya, and parts of Morocco. Their rivals were the caliphs in Baghdad, and the Fatimids were determined to take them down at all costs. They exploited the chaos that unfolded in Egypt and conquered it in 969.

The Fatimids controlled Egypt for the next century and a half. By the late 10th century, they had campaigned into Syria and the Levant and managed to take over the important cities on the eastern Mediterranean coast, including Jerusalem. Perhaps the most important legacy of the Fatimid dynasty is the city of Cairo, which was founded by the new rulers of Egypt. Cairo was adjacent to the Arab capital of Al-Fustat on the Nile Delta. Despite the fact that Egypt had technically been a recently conquered province, the Fatimids soon established it as the center of their power, shifting the capital city to the nearly constructed city. Cairo experienced a remarkable level of growth for the next few centuries, becoming a political, economic, and cultural powerhouse and one of the crown jewels of the Arab world.

The Fatimids were interesting rulers of Egypt, as their goal was to wage a war of revenge on the pretender Abbasid caliphs. This made their foreign policy very easy and predictable to dictate, though the Fatimids were never able to complete their war on the Abbasid caliphs despite establishing an empire that stretched from North Africa to the Levant and included territories in Sicily and Yemen.

Many different factors caused the decline of Fatimid Egypt, not just overextension and bureaucratic failure, as had been the case during the Tulunid and Ikhshidid rules. Although the Fatimids were Shi'a, the majority of Egypt's population continued to practice Sunni Islam. The Shi'a only constituted the elite class, which was in charge of the government, as well as pockets of believers that were scattered around the vast territories of the empire.

One may think religious differences were one of the primary reasons behind the gradual decline of the Fatimids. In fact, the dynasty is known for its tolerant treatment of the Jewish and Christian members of its population, who were beginning to constitute a minority. Religious minorities served in state offices and constituted an important portion of the bureaucrats. It was mainly during the reign of Fatimid Caliph al-Hakimi in the late 10th and early 11th centuries that they experienced persecution.

In addition, the Fatimid rule over Egypt saw the re-emergence of Egypt as one of the economic powerhouses of the Mediterranean. Cairo was conveniently located at a crossroads between the major trade routes that connected Europe with Asia. The city benefited immensely from this and grew to become a bustling metropolis by the beginning of the 12th century. The Fatimids implemented trade protectionist policies that helped boost domestic activity and attracted foreign merchants to Egypt.

The decline of the Fatimids was caused by two main factors. The first one was the decline of the caliph's authority after the death of Caliph al-Hakim, who had ambitious plans for the future of the realm after his death. Diverging from the traditional Fatimid understanding of the caliph as both a political and spiritual leader, al-Hakim decided to designate the two roles to two of his heirs. This threatened the ideology upon which the whole Shi'a branch of Islam had been centered around. It also created difficulties when it came to defining the Fatimid identity as a whole.

The court elites were against the proposed policy and were quick to organize a conspiracy after Caliph al-Hakim's death, killing both of his designated heirs. They installed his fifteen-year-old son, al-Zahir, on the throne. This meant that the courtiers, especially the viziers of the caliph, who essentially acted as prime ministers of the empire, gradually increased their power and influence over domestic politics. Though the Fatimid viziers were experienced bureaucrats who aimed to "serve the state," they were unable to effectively govern the realm without delegating a lot of autonomy to regional rulers, who eventually eclipsed them. Especially in the Levant and Syria, rulers of independent cities, supported by their loyal armies, rose up and challenged the authority of the Fatimid caliphs. This lasted all throughout the 11th century and was a leading factor behind the fall of the dynasty in the late 12th century.

The declining authority of the Fatimid caliph was accompanied by the appearance of a new threat in the region: the European Crusaders who wanted to claim the Holy Land from the "heathen" Muslims. The First Crusade, which succeeded in taking Jerusalem and the neighboring territories in 1099, weakened the Fatimids. The Crusaders managed to defeat the fragmented Seljuk Sultanate of Rum, which occupied much of Anatolia, and exploited the political instability of the Fatimids by going after independent urban centers in Palestine and Syria. They established themselves in Jerusalem and were a thorn in the side of the Fatimids for the next seventy years, launching multiple invasions into Egypt, which were repelled only due to the mistakes made by the Crusaders.

In 1153, the Crusaders captured Tyre, Ascalon, and Jaffa. They shifted their attention to the northeast, where the Muslim warlords in Syria were gaining ground. The Crusader conquests resulted in more instability in Egypt, leading to the assassination of the caliph and the emergence of Vizier Shawar as the ruler of Cairo. Central authority would not be restored by the Fatimids, as they failed to consolidate their forces and had to appeal to the Syrians to form an alliance against the Crusaders, who rampaged Cairo and the surrounding areas in the 1160s. The Fatimids eventually fell out with the Syrians, who wished to take over Egypt themselves. They proceeded to ask for help from none other than King Amalric I of Jerusalem, who quickly assembled a force and led another offensive into Egypt, this time with the aim of reinstating his former ally, Shawar, in Cairo.

In April of 1167, Nur ad-Din, the ruler of the Zengid dynasty of Syria under the Seljuks, sent a force led by General Shirkuh into Egypt, which managed to defeat the Fatimids and conquer the territory without much resistance. With Fatimid Vizier Shawar dead, the de facto control of Egypt was claimed by the Zengids, and the nephew of Shirkuh, Salah ad-Din Yusuf ibn Ayyub—better known in history as Saladin—was installed as the vizier. He served under the last Fatimid caliph, al-Adid, who was still the nominal ruler of the empire despite the fact that he held little to no political influence within his own realm.

The end of the Fatimid Caliphate came with al-Adid's death in September 1171. Salah ad-Din, who was still young at the time, took over control of Egypt, founding the Ayyubid dynasty, which would become one of the most powerful Muslim empires in history. Saladin would make a name for himself as one of the wisest and most successful leaders of his time.

The Ayyubid Sultanate

The Ayyubids marked the return of Egypt to its former glory, with the state achieving economic and political power like it had not seen for several centuries. Saladin was the main architect behind the success of the Ayyubids. He made the empire not only a center of Muslim resistance against the Crusaders but also a cultural and economic hub. Saladin adopted the title of sultan in 1174 after the death of Nur ad-Din, the prominent Zengid leader in Syria. As a Sunni Muslim, one of Saladin's chief policies was to realign Egypt, which had been ruled by the Shi'a elite for over a century, back to the rest of the Sunni world. By the late 12th century, the Abbasid caliph, who resided in Baghdad, was still the nominal leader of the Islamic world, though his power had greatly diminished. In

Anatolia and Mesopotamia, the Seljuk Turks were the most prominent Islamic power, though they themselves had experienced a long period of internal instability. Saladin's aim was to push back against the Crusaders, who were still barely holding onto their possessions in the Levant, and to gain control of the weaker Muslim regional powers that held major cities in Syria and Iraq.

Saladin had a very interesting personality. He was a devout Muslim who dedicated a lot of his time to learning, something that might explain many of his wise policies that contributed to the ascendancy of his sultanate to the top of the Islamic world. Although he was a fervent believer in the Muslim cause, including in waging the holy wars, Saladin was a tolerant ruler who greatly respected foreign and minority cultures and ways of life.

After establishing his power base in Cairo, Saladin proceeded to reinforce the Sunnis in Egypt, who constituted the majority of the Muslim population there, but did not persecute the Coptic Christians and Jews, who had been victims of some of the previous dynasties. He encouraged diversity within the territories he controlled and was an avid scholar of history and theology. Arguably, this was what distinguished him from the other prominent leaders of his time, most of whom were concerned with conquest and the glory that came with it instead of focusing on what their people needed.

Interestingly, Saladin's power was not concentrated in Egypt by the end of his reign. Instead, it was in Syria, where the sultan and most of his armies spent their time. Saladin was of Kurdish descent and an old ally of Nur ad-Din, so he was able to peacefully take over the city of Damascus in 1174 after the latter's death, coming into possession of one of the largest cities in the region. Saladin subsequently made the city his seat and transferred his power base to Syria, taking important centers such as Aleppo and pressuring the Crusaders for the next decade and a half.

When he took over a new territory, Saladin installed one of his kinsmen as its ruler, a practice that was aimed at making sure the lands were ruled by loyal subjects. This proved to be very effective in the short term, as Saladin consolidated his power in Egypt and asserted his control over the lands controlled by the Zengids. Abbasid Caliph al-Mustadi proceeded to "formally" recognize the suzerainty of the Ayyubid sultan over all of Egypt and Syria. Baghdad was still weak during Saladin's reign, but recognition from the nominal head of the Islamic world was of great symbolic importance.

The Ayyubid Sultanate reached its peak after Saladin decisively defeated the Crusader Kingdom of Jerusalem and its allies at the Battle of Hattin in 1187. The Crusaders had been a thorn in the side of the sultan, violating many ceasefire agreements that Saladin had struck to maintain security in the region and allow for the safe conduct of trade. At Hattin, Saladin broke the majority of the Crusaders' forces, rendering their defense of Jerusalem useless. He proceeded to take the city. Jerusalem was under Muslim rule for the first time after its loss during the First Crusade in 1099. Saladin treated the city's Christian inhabitants with tolerance. He did not resort to bloodshed like the First Crusaders had in 1099. He even allowed them a degree of freedom of worship and pilgrimage. The Third Crusade would be launched by European Christians after the fall of Jerusalem, though it would only achieve partial success and mark the beginning of a long and tenuous end of the Crusader States in the Levant, which continued to decline.

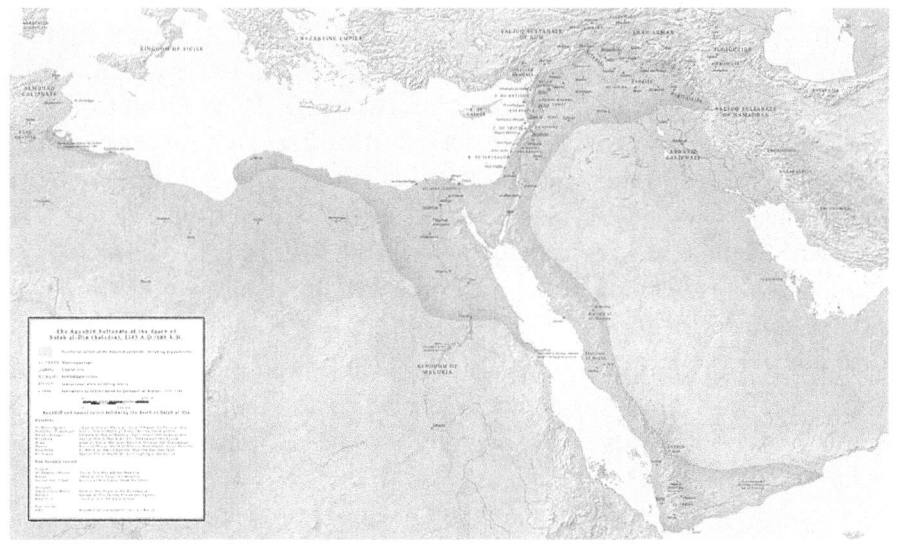

Map of the Ayyubid Sultanate under Saladin. [17]

Saladin consolidated many of the Muslim territories in the Near East under Ayyubid rule. He died in 1193 and was buried in Damascus. His death began the disintegration of his short-lived empire, as regional governors appointed by the Ayyubid sultan proceeded to defy central authority. The result was that the Ayyubid Sultanate was a decentralized state for about the next six decades. Succeeding sultans had to reconquer the lands that had been under the control of Saladin for themselves in order to emerge as sultans of both Egypt and Syria.

Sultan al-Malik al-Kamil, who ascended the throne in 1218 and reigned for twenty years, managed to restore some of the former glory of the Ayyubids, repulsing Crusader attacks on the Egyptian heartland during the Fifth Crusade. After years of campaigning, which had begun in 1217, the Ayyubids had to surrender the city of Damietta to the Crusaders, who had the upper hand in the war since the sultanate was on the brink of collapse. Their decision to continue pushing toward Cairo and refuse the generous peace terms offered by Sultan al-Kamil resulted in the annihilation of their army at the Battle of Mansurah in August of 1221. With his position undermined, al-Kamil was forced to give the control of Jerusalem back to the Crusader leader Frederick II, Holy Roman Emperor, during the Sixth Crusade (1228-1229).

The Mamluks

The disintegration of the Ayyubid Sultanate followed a series of succession disputes that had developed because of the increasing decentralization of power after Saladin's death. The next sultans were not powerful enough to maintain unity in the lands of the empire that stretched from Syria to the North African coast. By the time the Fifth Crusade managed to briefly gain back control of Jerusalem, the Ayyubids' fate was no longer in their hands. As was the case of the Fatimid dynasty's decline, the fall of the Ayyubids was essentially due to two factors. The Ayyubid Sultanate was basically gone by 1260, with only the Principality of Hama in Syria remaining under the control of the dynasty until 1341 when it was destroyed for good.

The first factor of the Ayyubids' decline stemmed from domestic problems. Ever since the reign of Saladin, an increasing number of Mamluk slave warriors were brought to the empire. They were the backbone of the Ayyubid military. Most Mamluks were ethnically Kipchak Turks who were Arabized after their conversion to Islam. Mamluk warriors were known for their loyalty and religious zeal. They were among the best fighters in the Islamic world.

Their status within the Ayyubid ranks underwent a significant transformation by the time of Sultan al-Salih, who ascended the throne in 1240. Al-Salih increasingly relied on the Mamluks. He bought them in large numbers and even promoted them within the military. One reason behind this was the increasing political instability in the region, which made it necessary to increase the army. Al-Salih also wished to create a quasi-personal force of Mamluk warriors, one that he would be able to personally control against any pretenders who happened to claim the Ayyubid throne. In doing so, Sultan al-Salih frequently quarreled with the Mamluk leadership, even if his warriors were instrumental in defending Egyptian lands from the Seventh Crusade (1248-1254), an unsuccessful attempt at saving the Crusader holdings led by King Louis IX of France.

Al-Salih's successor, al-Muazzam Turanshah, ascended the throne of a disintegrating empire in 1249. One of the policies of the new sultan was the promotion of the Arab Kurdish corps within his army rather than continued overreliance on the Mamluks, which constituted a significant force of Egypt's military at that point. In fact, there is evidence to suggest that the Mamluk corps enjoyed a degree of autonomy, pledging its support to the sultan who best utilized their services.

The new sultan's ambitious policy threatened their interests. Turanshah was assassinated by disenchanted Mamluk generals in May 1250. The Mamluks were in charge of the Ayyubid Sultanate, which they sought to transform into a militaristic polity where they would play a leading role. Aybak, a fellow Mamluk commander and an atabeg (the noble ruler) of one of the Ayyubid provinces, married the wife of former Sultan al-Salih, legitimizing the rule of the new overlords of Egypt and Syria. At least in Egypt, the short but effective rule of the Ayyubids had come to an end.

The Mamluk rebellion against their former Ayyubid masters transformed the political dynamics of Egypt, and Ayyubid authority in Syria was threatened by another factor: the Mongols. Rampaging their way through all of Asia, the Mongol Empire had recently run over Iran and reached Mesopotamia, where they put an end to the weak Abbasid Caliphate after taking Baghdad in 1258. With no Abbasid caliph to continue the succession of the de facto political and spiritual leadership of the Sunni Islamic world, anarchy was created in the region. Several armed struggles for survival and power broke out. The weak Crusaders were no longer a threat, losing their cities and fortresses during the second half of the 13th century.

The Mongols, though they themselves adopted Islam about halfway through their conquests, were the new faction to beat for the mastery of the Near East. Having taken Baghdad and controlling much of Iraq, they were a natural enemy to the Mamluks, who had designs on all of the territories conquered by Saladin. The Ayyubid Sultanate had lost most of its territories in Syria, meaning that the onus was on the former military slaves to organize a resistance against the Mongol war machine.

Depiction of a typical Mamluk warrior in heavy armor from medieval Egypt.[18]

The might of the Mamluks was best demonstrated in the Battle of Ain Jalut, which took place in September 1260 against the Mongols in the Jezreel Valley. Up until that point, the relations between the Mongols and the Mamluks had been tense, as characterized by the events leading up to the declaration of war. Sultan Qutuz, who had taken over Mamluk leadership, was insulted after Hulegu Khan, the ruler of the Mongols, sent him emissaries demanding his surrender. Qutuz had the envoys killed and their heads placed on one of the gates of Cairo to signal that his authority would not be undermined, especially by a foreign power. When the two armies met later that year, the Mongols, who had previously been virtually undefeated, suffered one of the most decisive defeats in their history. The Mamluk cavalry, consisting of both light horse archers and heavy shock troops, outmaneuvered the Mongols, who were renowned for their mastery of the horse. Mamluk General Baibars showed exceptional prowess in the battle, emerging as a hero. In time, he took over the Mamluk Sultanate for himself.

By 1260, the Mamluk Sultanate, with its center in Cairo, had successfully managed to inflict a serious defeat on the Mongols, who were never quite able to gain a firm hand in the Levant and suffered another decisive defeat against the Mamluks four decades later. With their victory and the subsequent takeover of Baibars, the state the former slave warriors had established in Egypt was slowly showing its true colors. Though it was ruled by the sultan, in reality, most power lay in the hands of the military generals. The Mamluks had been ethnic Turks who relied heavily on kinship ties and had especially strong tribal connections to their military leaders, whom they respected immensely. Conquest and victory were the main tools for legitimizing the new rulers of Egypt, which helps to explain the decades of relative prosperity that would be ushered in after the defeat of the Mongols. In some shape or form, the Mamluks continued to rule Egypt until the early 16th century, surviving a hurricane of domestic rebellions, revolts, and conspiracies while pushing back against foreign invaders.

Mamluk history is divided into two periods. The first one, spanning from the establishment of the Mamluk Sultanate in 1252 to the accession of Sultan Barquq in 1382, is known as the Bahri period. Bahri Mamluks were ethnically Kipchak Turks who had initiated the rebellion against the Ayyubids and constituted the most significant part of the Mamluk ruling elite until 1382. During their control of Egypt, the state reached the height of its power. After the victory at Ain Jalut, Sultan Baibars destroyed the remaining territories of the Crusader States in the Levant and added parts of Syria to the Egyptian empire. In the eyes of the Arab Muslims, the Mamluks had managed to save the Islamic civilization from the Mongol conquerors, who were too ruthless in their treatment of fellow Muslims and often utilized Christian mercenaries in their armies.

The symbolic role of the Mamluks as the protectors of the Islamic faith manifested itself after the Mongols deposed the last Abbasid caliph after they had seized Baghdad in 1258. They installed al-Mustansir, a member of the Abbasid family, as the new caliph in Cairo instead of the traditional seat of the caliphs at Baghdad. The caliphs enjoyed many privileges but held little actual political power in Mamluk affairs, which were dominated by powerful military commanders. Nevertheless, they were an important source of legitimacy for the Mamluk sultans, as they endorsed their actions and showed the people that the new masters of Egypt were zealous defenders of the faith. The caliphs in Cairo blessed the Mamluks since they sought to restore the old borders of the Egyptian empire and emerge as masters of Egypt, Syria, the Levant, and the western part of the Arabian Peninsula. In fact, Mamluk patronage of the cities of Mecca and Medina reaffirmed their commitment to defending what was sacred to Islam.

The Bahri Mamluks were eventually replaced by the Burji Mamluks, who were ethnically Circassian instead of Kipchak. By 1382, the ethnic element had been widely introduced in the domestic power struggles between the Mamluks. Mamluks of Circassian descent increasingly favored each other in succession disputes despite the fact that they did not possess enough military power to maintain the unity of the state.

The rising instability also coincided with an array of external factors that led to the gradual decline of Mamluk authority in the distant provinces of the empire. In the middle of the 14th century, Egypt was struck by the plague, which wiped out millions of its inhabitants and caused a shortage of men in different fields of economy, especially in agriculture. As a result, the Mamluks entered a brief era of crisis, something that was shared by the rest of the Near East and Europe since they, too, were decimated by the plague.

Economic turmoil made the domestic political situation increasingly chaotic, and the emergence of the Circassian Burji Mamluks coincided with the appearance of another formidable adversary in the region: the Timurid Empire. They were the continuers of the Turkic-Mongolic nomadic warrior tradition. The Timurids were led by their general, Tamerlane, who invaded Syria in the late 14th century. By the second decade of the 15th century, the Timurids had sacked the cities of Aleppo and Damascus, dealing a blow to the Mamluks, from which they never recovered. The Mamluks had to abandon their designs on the Levant and southeastern Anatolia, as the Anatolian Turkic beyliks vied for more power and dominance in the region.

In addition, by the end of the 15th century, the appearance of European maritime powers in the Red Sea and the basin of the Indian Ocean further challenged the economic interests of the Egyptians. Portugal was the first nation to develop new trade routes around Africa, and it began to monopolize the Indian trade routes that previously ran through the Muslim world. The Mamluk leaders, whose military power was a mere shadow of its former past, could do nothing but watch as their empire crumbled piece by piece.

Still, even if the 16th century marked the end of Mamluk dominance as the main power in the Near East, the social and cultural developments undertaken during their sultanate were significant in transforming and advancing the Islamic world. During the reign of the Mamluks, Egypt essentially adopted a role as the new center of the Arab world. Cairo had seen remarkable growth, emerging as both an economic and cultural powerhouse. Baghdad and Damascus still remained important Muslim cities, but they had been eclipsed by the Egyptian capital, which stood proudly as other major centers struggled in the hands of a diverse range of foreign invaders.

The Mamluks recognized their role in preserving one of the most important institutions in Islam, the caliphate, which had essentially been dissolved by the Mongols in 1258. Although the caliph they installed in Cairo was nothing but a symbolic figurehead, one has to understand that the existence of such a figurehead was significant in the Muslim world, which had been engulfed in centuries of peril. The way in which the Mamluks fused their Turkic warrior identity with their Islamic identity as the protectors of the Arab world was unique. Egypt increasingly adopted a distinct Arabic outlook.

The Mamluks utilized their position perfectly, supporting religious institutions in the country, which, in turn, granted legitimacy to its overlords. Many mosques and madrasas (Muslim schools) were founded by the Mamluks. These evolved over time and adopted new roles in Cairo and elsewhere. Though Cairo was by no means the intellectual center Baghdad had been during the Islamic Golden Age, it still produced a rich tradition of historiography. The Mamluks were, above all, conquerors, and it was important that their activities were adequately chronicled.

Generally speaking, the Mamluks were only somewhat tolerant toward the primarily Jewish and Christian religious minorities who dwelt in the empire. They recognized the bureaucratic experience of some Christian institutions, such as the Coptic Church, which stemmed from Egypt's centuries-long tradition of running a strong administrative system. Nevertheless, there were instances when religious minorities were persecuted and not allowed to publicly profess their faith. This only further accelerated the Arabization and Islamification of Egypt, which eventually completed its transformation from a predominantly Christian Greco-Roman state into an Islamic state.

Chapter Seven – The Ottomans and Early Modern Egypt

As we saw in the previous chapter, medieval Egypt underwent a profound transformation from a Byzantine province to an Arabized region. This period saw the return of Egypt as a renewed political and cultural center in an increasingly changing world, though this would only last for so long. By the beginning of the 16th century, Mamluk rule over Egypt and the other lands of the sultanate was quickly deteriorating as other powers were quickly gaining ground. This led to the Ottoman conquest of Egypt and the establishment of Egypt as an imperial province once again.

Ottoman Egypt

Beginning in the 14th century, the Ottoman Turks of Anatolia slowly expanded their influence. They took Constantinople in 1453, putting an end to the Byzantine Empire. The Ottomans focused their efforts on reinstating the borders of the old Eastern Roman Empire. They conquered much of the Balkans and consolidated their rule over Anatolia, with designs to expand farther to the southeast and push back against the successor states of the Timurid Empire.

By the beginning of the 16th century, their empire had come into conflict with another rising power, Safavid Persia, a Shi'a Muslim empire that managed to emerge as the most powerful Iranian state after the birth of Islam. With the next two giants of the Muslim world taking center stage, Mamluk Egypt, which had increasingly struggled for the past century, was slowly being sidelined. Weakened because of domestic and foreign conflicts, the Mamluks were busy trying to reestablish their dominance over the maritime trade routes of the Red Sea and the Indian Ocean against the Portuguese. Their days as masters of Egypt were numbered.

The Ottomans slowly but surely began eyeing the territories of the declining Mamluk Sultanate. In 1516, after achieving a temporary peace with the Safavid Persians, they started to look for a foothold in the northeastern Mamluk territories. The Mamluks were dependent on regional vassals who ruled parts of Syria on behalf of the Mamluk sultan. Struggling with an array of internal problems, the Mamluks were unprepared for the Ottoman assault, which came in August. The Ottomans mustered more than sixty thousand men and marched on Syria, where the Mamluks were forced to confront them with a similar-sized force. The outcome of the Battle of Marj Dabiq shocked the Islamic world and clearly signaled that the old days of Mamluk military dominance were gone.

The Mamluks had been slow to modernize, over-relying on their cavalry and archers. The Ottomans had an advantage due to their elite Janissary corps and their use of gunpowder weapons, which were effective in cutting down the Egyptians. Crucially, the Mamluks had invested everything they had in assembling an army that was supposed to stop the Ottomans. Sultan al-Ghawri had led the forces himself, though he was one of the casualties to fall on the battlefield, located several kilometers north of Aleppo. The routed Mamluk force tried to retreat to the Syrian city, which was under the control of one of the Mamluk vassals. However, they were denied entry since he had switched allegiance to the Ottomans. The humiliated surviving Mamluk forces had to retreat all the way to Egypt. They were never again in a position to resist the Ottomans.

In January 1517, the Ottomans defeated the Mamluk resistance throughout the Levant and marched on Cairo virtually unopposed. Due to the dwindling authority of the Mamluk Sultan Tuman Bay, they were able to quickly gain the loyalty of some of the Mamluk elite. The sultan himself fled south and put up a last stand near Giza. Selim the Great, the sultan of the Ottoman Empire who largely made his name with his successful military endeavors against the Safavids and Mamluks, put Tuman Bay to death in April 1517.

Egypt was again made an imperial province. It was subject to the authority of its overlords back in Istanbul, the name the Turks gave Constantinople after its conquest. For the next couple of centuries, the

Ottomans exploited the existing political and social problems in Egypt, which led to the disappearance of Egypt from the list of the world's leading states.

Khayr Bey, the Syrian leader who had betrayed the Mamluks, was installed as the first governor of Egypt and served until his death in 1522. Under the reign of Ottoman Sultan Suleyman the Magnificent, Egypt was officially integrated into the Ottoman Empire, with the administrative functions of its rulers clearly defined by imperial policy. The rulers of Egypt were made de facto viceroys, occupying a somewhat privileged position throughout the empire's provincial administration hierarchy. The viceroy, called *wali*, held the leading position in Ottoman Egypt. He was supported by an advisory body reminiscent of the *divan* (a high-ranking government ministry in several Muslim states), which served the same purpose for the sultan in Istanbul. Moreover, Egypt's administration was divided into four sub-provinces, each ruled by a designated *kashif*, who was also centrally appointed.

The Ottomans had to figure out what to do with the Mamluks, who still constituted a separate class of Egypt's population and had a distinct social status. The Ottomans understood the volatility of the Mamluk factions and knew that there existed a real possibility of exploiting it to pursue their own ends. If the Mamluk elites were left to fend for themselves, they had the capacity to organize a significant threat against foreign Ottoman rule, especially as new Mamluks arrived from the widespread slave trade. Thus, the Ottomans proceeded to involve many Mamluks in the complex government apparatus and even assigned certain Mamluk leaders to the position of kashif. Gradually, the Mamluks were transformed from the Arabized emirs to the Turkish beys. They continued to hold positions of power under Ottoman administrative structures.

Their military role took the biggest hit, as the old Mamluk regiments, which were based on the Turkic notion of loyalty to the war chieftains, were largely disbanded. The Ottomans kept a permanent garrison in Egypt, which made it difficult for individual Mamluks to consolidate enough power to permanently oust the new suzerains of Egypt and return the old ruling class back to the top. Nevertheless, the Mamluks slowly rose through the ranks of the Ottoman administration by the end of the 17th century, eventually retaking the power base that had been disrupted since 1517. Although they ascended back to the higher echelons of Egyptian politics, they did so with a modified role and status, something that would play a big role in the latter half of Ottoman control over Egypt.

Ottoman conquests reached their peak during the 16th century. In many cases, Egypt was used as a hub for future campaigns, which were directed both westward across the Mediterranean coast and southward up the Nile and by the Red Sea. By the end of the 1500s, the Ottomans had imposed their rule on the major centers of the Arabian Peninsula, benefiting immensely from controlling the trade routes that ran through their lands. The rule of the most distant provinces was often delegated to local regional dynasties and lords, as the Ottomans increasingly shifted their attention to battling both the Safavids and the Europeans.

By then, the Ottomans had begun to struggle with the classic issues that plagued the vast majority of empires that came before and after them. These problems were mainly caused by rapid overextension. As the Ottoman Empire began to encompass a diverse range of peoples, ethnicities, and cultures, its state apparatus was shown to be increasingly incompetent in dealing with the needs and demands of the different groups. This created domestic problems, which, coupled with the lack of strong, authoritative sultans, resulted in gradual cracks, which began to appear in the Ottoman Empire in the 17th century.

Interestingly, the tactics the Ottomans had implemented in Egypt in order to run the province smoothly proved to be deadly in the long term. Egypt experienced a period of stagnation, both economically and socio-culturally, as it lost its importance as one of the crown jewels of the Islamic world. Arabic centers, be it Mecca, Medina, Baghdad, Damascus, or Cairo, had always been the centers of the Islamic religion since the advent of the religion in the 7th century. The continuity of the Arabic civilization had been dependent on the strength of the caliphate and its successors. After the takeover by the Ottomans, who were ethnically Turks and not Arabs, the center of the Islamic civilization shifted to Istanbul, where the whole concept underwent a significant transformation. Despite being the capital of the strongest Muslim empire in the world, Istanbul by no means possessed a distinctively Islamic outlook. Since the age of the Roman Empire, it had been a melting pot of different cultures and peoples and one of the most important Christian cities in all of Christendom. Although Islamization continued under the Ottomans, both in Istanbul and in other non-Muslim territories of the empire, it slowly lost its Arabic flavor, resulting in the disenchantment of many who wished to see Islam and the Arab world return to its former glory.

Egypt, as the place with the most powerful recent sultanate before the rise of the Ottomans, increasingly became a center of resistance. Despite the efforts of the Ottomans to pit the Mamluks against each other, they still were important elites who had both enough means and legitimacy to mount a resistance. During the 17th and 18th centuries, challenges to Ottoman rule in Egypt were so frequent that governors were appointed from Istanbul on almost a yearly basis. Just as they had done in the past, Mamluk emirs would consolidate their support in one of the empire's regions and then act autonomously, largely defining the expectations and orders of the Ottoman government. Thanks to the influence the Mamluks held in the army, they were able to achieve de facto autonomy in Egypt multiple times in the 1600s and 1700s. In fact, the Mamluks began to be increasingly divided among themselves, leading to the creation of the Faqāriyyah (Faqari) and the Qāsimiyyah (Qasimi) factions. The former held important positions in the Ottoman army, while the latter were supported by local Egyptian forces.

By the end of the 18th century, the Ottoman Empire had increasingly shifted its attention to European affairs, resulting in more instability in Egypt. In the 1760s, the centrally appointed pasha had to flee Cairo, which was taken over by the Mamluks, which complicated the dynamics between the different prominent houses in Egypt. Ali Bey, a former Caucasian slave who wanted to avenge the death of his master Ibrahim Pasha, exploited the instability of the empire during the Ottoman-Russian War, which began in 1768. Taking over not only Ottoman Egypt but also territories in Syria, Arabia, and Yemen, Ali Bey emerged as the de facto independent ruler of Egypt for a brief spell. He managed to secure (at least temporarily) the loyalty of the prominent Mamluks in Egypt, who aided his designs by contributing thousands of warriors to his cause, which created many problems for the Ottoman government.

The old Mamluk ways of dominance through army diplomacy were slowly returning as Egypt slipped away from Ottoman control. The rebels even wanted to negotiate with Venice and Russia, two of the main rivals of the Ottoman Empire, to aid them in undermining Istanbul in favor of local self-governance. Eventually, this and other uprisings were dealt with by the Ottomans in one way or another. Ironically, the Ottomans themselves would manage to exploit the splintered Mamluk relationships and promote a faction that would oppose the rebels.

In short, by the late 18th century, more than two centuries of Ottoman rule over Egypt had demonstrated two things. Firstly, the influence of the Mamluks and the long-standing tradition of army diplomacy were still prominent factors in Egyptian politics, which was unstable and largely incohesive, with the Mamluks unable to mount a united effort against the Ottomans. Secondly, despite such disunity among the Mamluks, the Ottomans had been unable to institute sufficient mechanisms to turn Egypt into a stable province. This would best be demonstrated in 1798 when Egypt was invaded by none other than Napoleon Bonaparte.

The French Invasion

In 1798, Egypt suffered arguably the biggest crisis since it had become a province of the Ottoman Empire in 1517. A new foreign challenger appeared on Egyptian shores in early July of that year, landing at the coastal city of Aboukir, northeast of Alexandria. The French were already nearly ten years into the French Revolution and still engulfed in the chaos that came with it. At the time, France was fighting the conservative European alliance of the Second Coalition, which included its greatest rival, Great Britain. Napoleon Bonaparte, the leader of France, had been convinced that if an invasion of Britain was not feasible at the moment, a military campaign aimed at damaging British trade connections and impeding the economic dominance of the enemy had to be launched. This had been the justification behind the decision to invade and occupy Egypt since the French could threaten British trade interests in both the Mediterranean Sea and the Indian Ocean. Perhaps even more importantly, revolutionary France promised the return of prosperity and former glory to the once-strong but now war-torn Egypt.

Alongside the army, the French fleet that set sail from the port of Toulon included a group of learned scholars, which would guarantee the social and cultural revival of Egypt. This was consistent with the new universal ideas postulated by the French Revolution.

Leading the Armée d'Orient–as the French expeditionary forces that arrived in Egypt in July of 1798 were called–Napoleon managed to establish a secure landing and proceeded to Alexandria. The army included up to forty thousand soldiers and ten thousand sailors. The French forces managed to capture the Mediterranean island of Malta before reaching Egypt. Napoleon, believing that he marched in the footsteps of Alexander the Great, who had saved Egypt from the tyrannical rule of the Persians, was about to attempt the same. This time, the Egyptians had to be saved from their Mamluk overlords, whose militaristic designs had undermined the greatness of the Egyptians. Napoleon claimed that he came as a friend to the people of Alexandria, who were primarily Muslim.

He asserted that revolutionary France was the enemy of the enemies of the Muslims, such as the pope or the Knights of Malta, a successor order to the Knights Hospitaller, which had been one of the Catholic military orders during the Crusades. The French wanted to obtain the people's support, deciding to move quickly through Egypt and advance on Cairo next. They understood that the French fleet was of no match to the British.

On July 20th, Napoleon's forces engaged with a twenty-thousand-strong Mamluk army led by Murad Bey and Ibrahim Bey, two Mamluk chieftains who had jointly ruled Egypt for the Ottomans. The Battle of the Pyramids unfolded at the village of Imbaba (Embabeh). The pyramids were about ten miles away from the site of the battle, but the French general, who emerged victorious from the engagement, insisted that it bear the name of the great monuments. On July 25th, Napoleon managed to occupy Cairo as well. When his fleet was finally caught by the British and suffered heavy losses at the Battle of the Nile, which took place in early August, Napoleon was essentially forced to consolidate his power on land, as his support base had been almost eliminated. He established a temporary occupation administration in Cairo. He knew he had to act cautiously if he wanted to reach his desired goals in the region.

Although Napoleon claimed to have liberated the people of Egypt from tyrants, the regime he set up in Cairo was nothing short of repressive of any instances of Egyptian nationalism. The French general imposed his own rule on Egypt, placing many of his officers in positions of power to maintain order. Napoleon believed that the key to governing Egypt lay in the religious elite—the ulama—who played a leading role in the establishment of popular councils and assemblies that were supposed to boost representation. Though the French protected Islam as a fundamental building block of Egyptian society, Napoleon was insistent on granting minorities several fundamental freedoms. During the first six months of the new occupation administration, the Copts were granted equal status in the spirit of the French Revolution.

Napoleon, who was effectively isolated from the rest of France and blockaded by the British, threw a lavish celebration on the anniversary of the proclamation of the French Republic in September, complete with a military parade and gunshots. Napoleon made sure to convince the Egyptian people that liberation could only be achieved if the people followed his leadership. The celebrations were also meant to demonstrate French might and symbolize the toppling of the old regime, especially since they followed the declaration of war by Ottoman Sultan Selim III earlier in September 1798. France was now officially at war with the Ottoman Empire, but this had always been the plan. Istanbul, where the echoes of the French Revolution had not been heard as loud as in other parts of Europe, remained under the conservative Ottoman regime that wanted Napoleon out of what it considered its province.

The Egyptians' reception of the newly imposed occupation regime was not at all peaceful. Rebellions, acts of sabotage, and protests were common against the French invaders. Different groups struck French supply points and tried to weaken the occupiers ever since their blitzkrieg of Cairo in July. The Revolt of Cairo, which took place in October 1798, was brutally suppressed by the French forces. They fired their artillery from the city's citadel on the rebel forces, killing thousands in the process. In this light, it is clear why Napoleon's next step was to invade Ottoman Syria. The situation in Egypt was becoming more chaotic. Amidst protests and rebellions from the people and the looming British threat, which came from Upper Egypt, Napoleon chose to confront the Ottomans by taking the fight to them in February 1799.

However, the French invasion of Syria did not produce the results Napoleon had wanted. Initially, the offensive was able to defeat the Ottoman resistance in the Palestine region, taking the city of Jaffa, where Napoleon proceeded to implement similar administrative reforms as he had done in Cairo. In March, the army laid siege to Acre, an important historical site and one of the most fortified strongholds in all of Syria, but the French were unable to take it after two months of trying. Fearing that he would be cut off by the Ottomans, who had sent a naval force to establish a bridgehead at the delta, Napoleon decided to abandon his ambitious plans. The French retreated from Syria back to Cairo, having suffered up to four thousand casualties, which included wounded soldiers and those dead to the plague.

Their situation was getting desperate. The next few months saw only a further escalation of the conflict, with multiple engagements against the Ottomans and the British, as well as constant rebellions from the locals. Napoleon, terrified of the possibility that he would be surrounded by hostile forces, decided to flee Egypt altogether in August, delegating command to his deputy, Jean-Baptiste Kléber. On August 22nd, Napoleon, some of the other members of the French command, and French scientists who had accompanied the expedition quietly boarded the frigate *Muiron* and set sail from Egypt, somehow slipping past the British and reaching France by October.

The French forces felt abandoned, and rightfully so. Commander Kléber told his soldiers that Napoleon would return, but he negotiated a surrender and the evacuation of the French forces with the Ottomans and the British. The British refused. Kléber put up a last stand at Heliopolis, defeating the Ottoman army on March 20th, 1800, but the future of revolutionary France in Egypt was in tatters. In 1801, the French forces, pressed from all sides in Alexandria and Cairo, surrendered, and the brief French occupation of Egypt came to an end.

Despite its brevity, the French occupation was important because it established a precedent for early modern Egypt. Centuries of Mamluk and Ottoman rivalry had left the volatile region to deal with a power vacuum. Under Napoleon, Egypt was directly made a subject of broader European interests. As an old civilization but a struggling nation, Egypt could be easily exploited by the imperialist designs of the Europeans. They were aware of its rich culture and history, as well as its role as part of the Greek, Roman, and Muslim worlds.

This was best demonstrated by the fact that Napoleon was accompanied by a group of scholars who wished to study Egypt and explore its mysterious nature. The French discovered the Rosetta Stone, which allowed us to decipher Egyptian hieroglyphs and hugely contributed to our understanding of ancient Egyptian history. An entire new discipline of the study of Egypt—Egyptology—appeared in Europe at the beginning of the 19th century, with more and more scientists attracted to the possibility of uncovering the secrets of Egypt. Egypt thus reentered the public consciousness in Europe.

Early Modern Egypt

With the Treaty of Amiens, signed in March 1802, Britain and France made peace, which would last for just over a year. The treaty also included points about the return of Egypt to the Ottomans from the British. However, with the Europeans gone and the Mamluks greatly weakened by the French, the question of what to do with the province became of great importance to the Ottoman Empire. If anything, the defeat of the French had only put this question to the forefront while perpetuating the rivalry between the Ottomans and the Mamluks. Istanbul did not want the Mamluks back in charge of the province and appointed Koca Hüsrev Mehmed Pasha, the admiral of the Ottoman navy, as the new governor. The fighting continued under Mehmed Pasha's leadership, who was in charge of the Ottoman occupation forces that fought against the Mamluks.

One of the main contingents of the roughly seven-thousand-strong army was from Ottoman Albania. The leader of the Albanian contingent was a man named Muhammad Ali, who had distinguished himself during the 1801 campaign against the French and had made important contacts with Egypt's religious elite. Having gained a degree of popular support by 1805 and closely witnessing the unfolding of the chaotic activities between the Mamluks and the Ottomans, Muhammad Ali exploited the situation and seized control of Egypt for himself. This marked the beginning of a new era in Egypt's history, as a new dynasty would rule Egypt for most of the 19th century. Nominally, Egypt would continue to be a province of the Ottoman Empire, but the regime established by Muhammad Ali would be the first one under which Egyptian national awakening would begin to take place.

Portrait of Muhammad Ali.[19]

Sultan Selim III of the Ottoman Empire reluctantly recognized Muhammad Ali as the next *wali* or viceroy in Egypt. The sultan had been a largely unpopular figure, hoping to reform and modernize his empire, which was lagging behind compared to other European powers. He knew that he did not possess enough resources to oppose Muhammad Ali, who was not only backed by his loyal forces but also supported by the Egyptian ulama.

The new viceroy of Egypt slowly consolidated his rule over his new domain. The main opposition he had to face came from the Mamluk elite of Egypt, who weren't about to relinquish their control after centuries of rule. Sporadic fighting between individual Mamluk leaders and Muhammad Ali's forces continued until 1811. On March 11th, 1811, the viceroy of Egypt invited many prominent Mamluk leaders to a special event at the Cairo Citadel, a historic part of the city constructed by Saladin, to celebrate the beginning of a military expedition into Arabia, which was to be headed by his son, Tusun Pasha. The Mamluk leaders who appeared at the citadel were ambushed and killed by the forces loyal to Muhammad Ali. The next few months saw the elimination of other pockets of Mamluk resistance. Muhammad Ali managed to eliminate his main political opponent in Egypt and set his eyes on establishing a dynasty in Cairo that was to repeat the achievements of Egypt's most prosperous days.

The regime established by Muhammad Ali was somewhat unique, and not only because it was, largely speaking, in opposition to the central Ottoman authority in Istanbul. Ruling Egypt until his death in 1848, Muhammad Ali managed to consolidate his rule over the region like no other figure had done over the past few centuries. Since the Ottoman conquest, Egypt had been a constant, unstable battleground between the local Mamluk factions, who vied for power between themselves, and the Ottomans, who wished to impose imperial authority over Egypt. Now, with both forces significantly weakened, Muhammad Ali was essentially in charge of a semi-autonomous country all by himself and proceeded to implement many important changes that would be accepted by the Egyptian people. Muhammad Ali focused on gaining as much support from the people as possible and presented himself as the savior of Egypt. He began a process of its cultural and sociopolitical revitalization, which accelerated Egypt's development until it was taken over by the British in the late 19th century.

The image of Muhammad Ali as a suitable and strong leader of Egypt was reinforced from early on, ever since his involvement in the campaigns against the French. After becoming viceroy, he managed to beat the Europeans again in 1807. This time, the British invaded Alexandria as part of the British-Ottoman War, hoping to establish a base of power in the Mediterranean and disrupt French interests in the region since they were still at war with Napoleon. The Fraser Expedition, which was tasked with taking Alexandria, succeeded in March of 1807 but was unable to progress farther inland, being decisively defeated by Muhammad Ali's forces and forced to evacuate Egypt altogether. This made Muhammad Ali's claim as a defender of Egypt even stronger and helped him consolidate his position.

After the elimination of the Mamluks in 1811, Muhammad Ali, acting on behalf of the Ottoman Sultan Mahmud II, sent a force from Egypt into Arabia with the aim of recapturing the holy cities of Mecca and Medina, which had been taken by the reformist Wahhabi Muslim group. For the next two years, Muhammad Ali's forces campaigned mostly in the region of Hejaz on the western coast of Arabia, successfully defeating the Wahhabis and reinstating the sultan's rule over Arabia. In 1816, another expedition focused on consolidating rule in the central-eastern part of Arabia. It was led by Muhammad's son, Ibrahim, and was also successful. Ottoman control of the region was thus reestablished, largely thanks to the efforts of Egypt's viceroy.

In 1820, Muhammad Ali campaigned up the Nile River in northern Sudan. He faced firm resistance from the local Arabized population but was able to defeat them with a relatively small army of about five thousand men who possessed superior military technology. The conquest of Sudan not only made Muhammad Ali the master of the East African slave trade, which was used to replenish army contingents with fresh warriors, but also equipped his successors with a foundation for further expansion to the south.

As the viceroy's forces were converging on the Sudanese positions, Muhammad Ali got word about a new crisis in the Ottoman Empire, which had been caused by the quest for independence in Greece. The Ottomans ruled a multi-ethnic empire and had to deal with outbreaks of nationalist movements throughout its European lands, most notably in Greece, which rebelled in 1821. Greek revolutionaries were successful at defeating the Ottomans during the first phase of the struggle, prompting Mahmud II to call for Muhammad Ali's help in quelling the rebellion. Egypt's ruler, who was promised control of the island of Crete, sent an expeditionary force of sixteen thousand soldiers to the Aegean, led by his son, Ibrahim. Ibrahim Pasha was able to suppress the rebellion at Crete and proceeded to invade the southern Greek region of Morea at the request of the Ottoman high command in 1825.

As the Egyptian forces made ground against the Greek nationalists, European powers intervened against the Ottoman Empire and provided military and financial support to Greece, which swung the war effort. In October 1827, a combined British, French, and Russian navy engaged with the Ottoman-Egyptian fleet at the Battle of Navarino and achieved a decisive victory. Half of Egypt's navy, built up by the efforts of Muhammad Ali himself, was sunk. He had to withdraw his forces from Greece, and the European powers guaranteed Greek independence with the Treaty of London of 1827.

The defeat in Greece was the first major setback Muhammad Ali faced since he had emerged as the viceroy of Egypt in the early 19th century. Not only had he won all other important military engagements throughout his tenure as the wali, but he had also initiated a series of reforms that fundamentally transformed Egyptian society. Since the early days, he had envisioned the creation of an independent Egyptian state ruled by himself and his heirs, though he recognized that the present state of the Egyptian economy and society would not allow this goal to materialize. With the Mamluks defeated and the ulama on his side, his reforms sought to strengthen central authority. Muhammad Ali first began to change the financial capabilities of Egypt, introducing a new tax system that increased the government's revenue. The money that flowed in was invested into different sectors of the Egyptian economy, primarily in agriculture and domestic industry.

The old Mamluk nobility was stripped of many of their lands, which were redeveloped with the introduction of new irrigation systems. Muhammad Ali pursued a protectionist trade policy, compelling local producers to sell goods to the Egyptian government, which were later redistributed in the domestic market and put up for exports. Egyptian farmers benefited immensely, focusing their work on the production of crops like cotton. Muhammad Ali also invested heavily in the development of local arms production as one of the pillars of Egypt's newborn industry. In the mid-1820s, factories in Cairo produced gunpowder weapons, while Alexandria was the base of production for Egypt's navy, most of which would be destroyed at Navarino. The ruler's extensive building projects were supported by the corvée slave labor system, which greatly reduced the costs of such endeavors.

Despite his conservative views for the future of Egypt, which was to be an independent, Islamic, and militarily strong nation, Muhammad Ali looked to Europe when it came to initiating many of his reforms. He financed the trips of many promising students, officials, scientists, and officers to different European countries. He was able to use their experience to create a solid Egyptian bureaucracy to combat many of the problems that had existed in the country since the days of the Mamluks. Administrative reforms were aimed at making Egypt easier to govern, and they included the division of Egyptian territories into smaller administrative units. Many European experts were invited to come to Egypt, establish schools and professional colleges, and share their expertise in different fields, such as in the military, industry, or medicine. Efforts to boost secular education in the country paid off, with growing literacy rates and increasing access to foreign knowledge among the Egyptian population. Many aspects of Egypt that came to characterize Egypt during the 20th century can be traced to the efforts of Muhammad Ali, who managed to revitalize the country after centuries of turmoil.

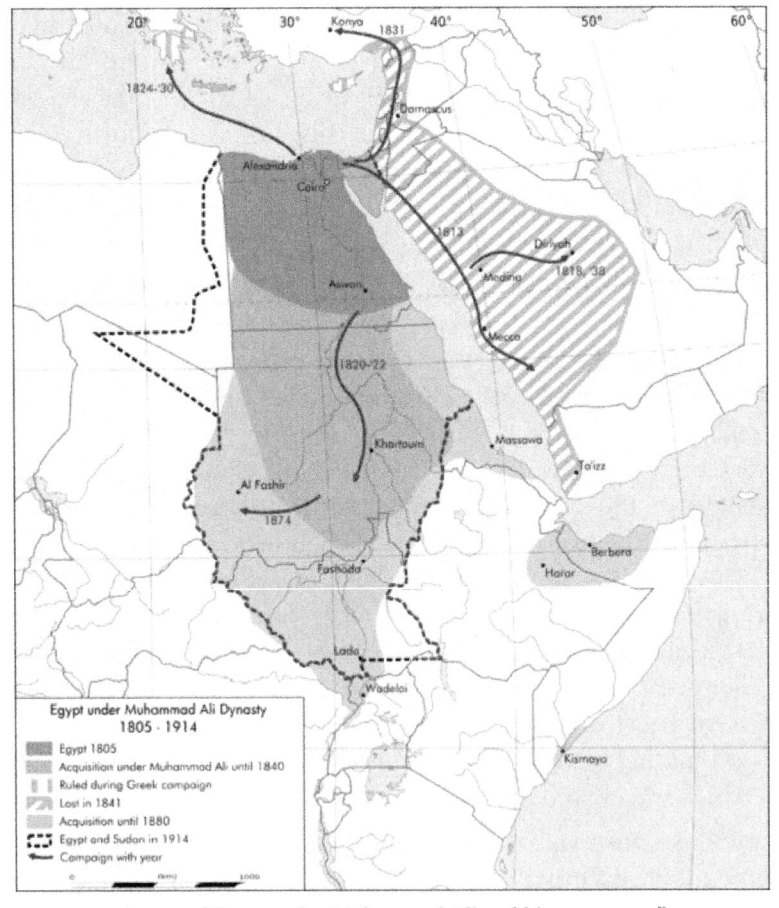

A map of Egypt under Muhammad Ali and his successors.[20]

Dynastic Decline

By the 1830s, Muhammad Ali had been at the forefront of Egyptian political life for about three decades. He was immensely popular among the people, who commended him for his effective policies and pragmatic approach to the state of affairs. However, the viceroy was still deeply upset about the fate of his forces in Greece. He felt that the Ottoman high command had been too incompetent to wage a war and felt betrayed by Istanbul, to which he still owed allegiance. In addition to losing much of his army and navy in Greece, Muhammad Ali had also been promised Crete, where the Ottomans were losing ground. As both compensation and an act of recognition for his efforts, Muhammad Ali requested control of the Ottoman province of Syria from Istanbul, a request that was promptly denied by the central government. Justifying his actions due to an ongoing conflict he had with the Ottoman governor of Acre, Abdullah Pasha, Muhammad Ali mustered up his army and marched on Ottoman Syria in October 1831.

His own ambitious imperial designs aside, control of Syria and the Levant would have given Muhammad Ali access to well-developed local markets, allowing him to extract taxes from the locals and reinvest the money into Egypt, his power base. More importantly, the Egyptian viceroy was cautious about the position of the sultan vis-à-vis his designs of dynastic rule over Egypt. Since the emergence of Muhammad Ali, the Ottoman policy regarding Egypt had been that of tacit agreement. The Ottomans granted the viceroy a virtual blank check regarding the situation in Egypt as long as the province was stable and Ottoman rule remained unthreatened.

The illusion of Ottoman-Egyptian friendship came to an end when Ali's forces laid siege to Acre and captured one of the centers of the Syrian province after six months in May 1832. Making their way through the Levant, Muhammad Ali's armies scattered any Ottoman resistance. By the end of the year, the control of the Syrian territories was firmly in the hands of the Egyptians after they emerged victorious at the Battle of Konya against a large Ottoman force in December. The viceroy's son, Ibrahim Pasha, already an experienced commander, was able to defeat an Ottoman army three times the size of his, thanks to the superior quality and discipline of his troops. Egypt's military had become increasingly modernized and was closer to European standards than the force fielded by the Ottomans. The main reason behind this had been the reforms of Muhammad Ali.

After their decisive victory at the Battle of Konya in December 1832, Egyptian forces under Ibrahim Pasha had the opportunity to march on Istanbul. However, Muhammad Ali, wary of provoking European intervention, framed the conflict as a quest for territorial control rather than a rebellion against the Ottoman sultan. The war concluded in 1833 with the Treaty of Kütahya, which granted Muhammad Ali control of Crete, the Hijaz, and Syria under nominal Ottoman sovereignty. Full Egyptian independence was not achieved, as the sultan refused to concede this.

For the next five years, the situation in the eastern Mediterranean was especially tense, as Muhammad Ali knew that the Ottomans did not yet have the resources to muster up another force that would be capable of stopping him. By the spring of 1838, he was enjoying his position and believed that he had the upper hand.

In June 1839, the Egyptians, led by Ibrahim Pasha, managed to achieve another decisive victory over the Ottomans at Nezib, defeating the bulk of their forces. With Sultan Mahmud II passing away soon after the disastrous battle, his young son, Abdülmecid, ascended the throne amidst a domestic crisis. Fearing that the potential collapse of the Ottoman Empire was against their imperial interests, the European powers again intervened. Muhammad Ali was offered partial autonomy over Egypt and the establishment of dynastic rule over the province if it continued to be under Ottoman rule. In exchange, he had to withdraw from Syria and stop the civil war. Muhammad Ali reluctantly agreed but only after the British threatened to launch an attack on his coastal territories, including on Alexandria.

The 1840s marked a terrible end for Muhammad Ali, who became increasingly paranoid and unfit to rule. Forced to come to terms with the fact that the most he could get out of the sultan was limited autonomy, the question of who would take over after Muhammad Ali hung in the air. Ibrahim Pasha, his designated successor, was suffering from an illness. After about three decades of development, Egypt had plateaued. Constant wars had depleted its treasury, and the country was facing a severe crisis.

Muhammad Ali died in 1849. His son, Ibrahim, who had taken over as the next wali the previous year, died in late 1848, with the news never reaching his father. Instead, Muhammad Ali's eldest grandson, Abbas, took over as the wali of Egypt in 1848, marking the beginning of a long and gradual decline of the dynasty.

The absence of a strong and charismatic ruler like Muhammad Ali took a toll on Egypt. Abbas I, who reigned until 1854, was a reactionary anti-Westerner who wanted to strengthen the traditional Islamic institutions in the country and tacitly acquiesced to Ottoman suzerainty. Only Sudan remained under his control, and later members of the dynasty would limit their military endeavors to central-eastern Africa. Abbas's reign can be viewed in light of the post-1848 conservative reaction to the liberal revolutions that had broken out that year all over the world. The Ottoman Empire had been trying to modernize with the Tanzimat movement since the late 1830s, and the Egyptian ruler was one of the main critics of the Turkish liberals.

Abbas was succeeded by Sa'id Pasha, the fourth son of Muhammad Ali, whose term as viceroy would last until 1863. He is best remembered for brokering a deal in 1856 with the French about the construction of the Suez Canal. According to the agreement, the French obtained the right to run the canal for ninety-nine years after its opening. The advantages of completing such a project seemed obvious to the many nations involved in the canal's construction. The British opposed the opening of the canal, acknowledging its potential to attract international traffic and undermine the key maritime routes in the Atlantic and the Indian Oceans controlled by Britain.

The work on the Suez Canal was completed under Sa'id Pasha's successor, Ismail, the son of Ibrahim Pasha and the grandson of Muhammad Ali. He became the viceroy in 1863. Ismail Pasha faced a lot of problems at the time of his accession, as Egypt was facing a serious economic crisis and was overly dependent on its cotton exports, which had boomed after the demand for the product had increased since the start of the American Civil War in 1861. Egypt had initially benefited from the disrupted market, as it became the premier exporter of the commodity for a brief period, but it had to accommodate for the lowering of cotton prices after the end of the conflict in the US in 1865. The opening of the Suez Canal in 1869, after years of artificially created delays and stalemates in negotiation, brought a breath of fresh air for Ismail Pasha, as the project instantly attracted international attention.

Much of Ismail Pasha's activities were directed toward reinforcing his own image as a strong ruler of a prosperous Egypt. The completion of the Suez Canal and the lavish celebrations that were thrown to mark its opening demonstrated the greatness of his rule. Two years before the opening, Ismail Pasha formally obtained the title of khedive from the

Ottoman sultan, an honorific that had originated in Persia and had been used to refer to important viziers. Muhammad Ali had been referred to as khedive during his lifetime, though this had not been officially part of his title under the sultan. The fact Ismail Pasha obtained the title shows the special status the viceroy of Egypt would play in the Ottoman Empire, as he would be distinct from all the other governors. The title came with a limited set of privileges, and Egypt was subsequently referred to as the Khedivate of Egypt.

Egypt resumed its military activities under Ismail Pasha. However, these campaigns did not resemble those of Muhammad Ali, neither in scale nor in the outcome. The conflicts were constrained to the African territories south of Egypt in modern-day Sudan and beyond. Egyptian forces managed to extend Egypt's boundary as far south as the region of Darfur in 1874, taking control of the slave and ivory trade routes that ran through its lands after defeating resistance from the local Africans. Egyptians also made their way into Ethiopia in the following years, taking the city of Harer with hopes of establishing firmer control over the Red Sea, but they were never able to impose firm control over the Ethiopian people.

The roots of the partial military failure in central-eastern Africa lay in the social and political developments that emerged in Egypt by the latter half of Ismail Pasha's rule. The lower echelons of Egypt's population were in turmoil. Muhammad Ali's agricultural reforms had led to the concentration of Egypt's arable lands in the hands of wealthy owners, including the dynastic house itself, leading to widespread poverty among the peasants. The peasants also had to serve in the military or as corvées in state-financed public projects, which took a great toll on the physical conditions of the population.

Decades of frequent conflicts also affected the composition of the army, one of the pillars of the state envisioned by Muhammad Ali, where the old Turkish elite—remnants of the Mamluk influence in Egypt—was increasingly being replaced by ethnically Egyptian forces. Native members of the army believed that the Turkish officers had been unjustly favored by the Egyptian leadership, adding to the negative attitudes against the government of Ismail Pasha.

Moreover, by the late 19th century, European liberal ideas had deeply penetrated the Muslim world, including in Egypt. The Ottoman Empire had already experimented with liberalization with the Tanzimat reforms, though the project lacked widespread enthusiasm in Istanbul and was only partially successful, further complicating the sociopolitical dynamics in the empire. A similar situation persisted in Egypt under the khedive, where an advisory body, the Assembly of Delegates, had been instituted by the viceroy. Though the local intelligentsia who subscribed to Western ideals constituted a small part of the overall assembly, these pro-Western attitudes affected Ismail Pasha, who was hoping for an economic miracle after Egypt had greatly exhausted its productive capabilities.

Financial troubles forced the viceroy's government to seek help from external sources. The public debt was rising uncontrollably. After the accession of Ismail Pasha, Egypt's debt had increased more than tenfold. A special commission comprised of European experts and bureaucrats was created to work on the issue. It was granted a lot of control over Egypt's fiscal affairs, something that was another hit to the viceroy's authority. He publicly accused Western forces of colluding together to topple his rule in early 1879. He dismissed the European ministers who had been working to fix some of the financial issues that faced the country.

We should not forget that despite all its looks, Egypt was still an Ottoman province, so the sultan technically had the final say on matters, even if Ottoman sultans chose to let the khedives be on their own. The commotion created in the late 1870s was not received well in Istanbul, where the conservative Sultan Abdulhamid II had just succeeded to the throne in 1876. Under pressure from Britain and France, who disapproved of Ismail Pasha's financial mismanagement and its impact on European interests in Egypt, Ottoman Sultan Abdülhamid II formally dismissed Ismail in June 1879. This was not a coup but rather a peaceful transfer of power orchestrated by European powers. Ismail's son, Muhammad Tawfiq, was installed as the new khedive, ensuring greater European influence over Egypt's governance and finances.

Egypt under the British

The deposing of Ismail Pasha led to chaos in Egypt. The country became increasingly polarized on the matter of European involvement in its affairs. A portion of the population advocated for more liberal reforms from the khedive. However, they were opposed by the majority of Egypt's population, as well as the major interest groups in the country's politics.

Being against both the despotic rule of the viceroy and the infringement of Egyptian national interests by foreigners, an Egyptian nationalist movement began to take shape in 1879. Many chief officers of the

Egyptian army, led by Colonel Ahmed Urabi, were members of the nationalist bloc. The officers had struggled greatly during the 1870s, especially since the unsuccessful Egyptian-Ethiopian War led to the reduction of government funding for the military, which left thousands unemployed. The size of the army shrunk considerably, as it mostly affected ordinary soldiers who were ethnic Egyptian Arabs, contrary to the leadership corps of officers, who were ethnic Circassians, Turks, or Albanians. Aside from the military, most Egyptians felt disenchanted. They believed that the existing social and political order unjustly favored foreigners and that the heavy tax burden had forced many into extreme poverty.

As the British and French ministers sought to implement measures that would have relieved Egypt from some of its public debt, they continued to increase their influence in the country. Khedive Tawfiq Pasha exerted little influence, as the Ottoman government's stance regarding its policies in Egypt was ambiguous. Meanwhile, nationalist officers, led by Ahmed Urabi, were in talks with other leading Egyptian nationalists who had been involved in the previous ministerial cabinet and had demonstrated their stances in the Assembly of Delegates, which had been dissolved a few years earlier. By pressuring the feeble khedive, Urabi and his followers were able to impose an ultimatum on Tawfiq Pasha about when he had to form a new pro-Egyptian government. In the summer of 1881, the viceroy demanded that the military contingent led by Urabi leave the capital, something that the latter refused to do. Political chaos continued for the rest of the year.

Fearing that the instability would damage their interests in the region, Britain and France decided to intervene on the side of the khedive, sending their warships to the Egyptian coast in the spring of 1882. The khedive moved to the coastal city of Alexandria, believing that the Europeans would best defend him there. The nationalists tried to rouse public support for their cause, emphasizing that European intervention would bring nothing but problems. The Egyptian state apparatus collapsed and was ended by the nationalists by the summer. They began to institute a series of changes to get rid of the Western presence in the country. There was fighting in the streets, and foreigners were harassed in both Cairo and Alexandria.

Commanded by Admiral Beauchamp Seymour, the British navy opened fire on Alexandria on July 11th, shelling the city, where the supporters of the khedive and Urabi clashed against each other. The bombardment resulted in hundreds of casualties, including civilians, prompting the retreat of the nationalist contingents from Alexandria. From this point on, there was no turning back. The British and the French planned a combined military intervention on land against the nationalists and landed in northern Egypt in late summer. Ahmed Urabi's forces were defeated by the British in September 1882 at the Battle of Tel El Kebir, some one hundred kilometers north of Cairo. The British then marched into Cairo and occupied it.

At the height of European imperialism, Egypt was taken over by the British. The move came at an increasingly tense global moment, as the major superpowers of the world were trying to maintain a balance of power and not infringe on each other's spheres of influence too much in the hopes of avoiding a destructive war. The Ottoman Empire was weak. It had struggled for decades to impose central authority over Cairo, so the British were left without any real resistance at first. They proclaimed that they were acting on behalf of keeping the peace in the region. Tawfiq Pasha was still the khedive, though he would become increasingly dependent on the foreigners.

Instability in Egypt meant instability with the Suez Canal and possible problems with the conduct of trade. Problems with trade meant the disruption of the world's increasingly globalized economy. More importantly, though, control of the Suez meant the traffic that went through the canal would benefit the power that controlled it. This, in addition to expanding their colonial holdings in Africa, had been the chief motivation behind the British to take over Egypt in 1822.

At first, the British were unsure of what to do with Egypt's governance. It was clear that leaving it in the hands of the weak khedive was dangerous and risky. On the other hand, the British would come under international scrutiny if their control over Egypt was more obvious than that of the Ottomans, who were still the nominal suzerains of the province. For instance, the French, who had aided the British in neutralizing the nationalist threat in 1882, were critical after the British proceeded to disregard them in relation to Egyptian financial affairs. Both parties jointly contributed to running the Egyptian economy and financial sector as part of the Caisse de la Dette (the Commission of Public Debt). After years of conflict between the French and the British diplomats, they agreed to involve other European representatives in the commission to balance out their interests. At the 1888 Convention of Constantinople, European powers met at the Ottoman capital and agreed on a treaty that guaranteed the secure entry of all ships through the canal. The convention was led by Britain, and the signatories included the Ottoman Empire, France, Russia, Germany, Austria-Hungary, Spain, Italy, and the Netherlands.

Khedive Tawfiq Pasha.[21]

Interestingly, no representatives from Khedive Tawfiq's government were present at the negotiations even though the Egyptian government owed many shares in the French-run Suez Canal Company, something that Ismail Pasha had negotiated in the 1860s before the opening of the canal. Since the British takeover, Egypt had been administered by Evelyn Baring, Earl of Cromer. Lord Cromer was London's direct representative and, in many respects, a viceroy, as he was concerned with the internal affairs of Egypt. The Egyptian cabinet of ministers, which was still technically in charge of the country, continued to operate under Lord Cromer's watchful eye. The Egyptian ministers had to coordinate their policies and executive decisions with the British, leading to instances when the interests of the two clashed, resulting in the dismissal and resignation of many Egyptian ministers.

A British Protectorate

The late 19th and early 20th centuries marked the peak of European imperialism. European powers imposed pseudo-autocratic regimes in their colonies and overseas dependencies, exploiting the native population for their own economic or military interests and pitting the different groups in the country against each other. Meanwhile, anti-European sentiments and protests against their fruitless and perilous regimes led to the development of nationalism in many societies, a process that stretched decades in certain places.

The British involved themselves more in the domestic affairs of Egypt in the 1890s. In 1892, Abbas II succeeded Tawfiq Pasha as the next khedive of Egypt. The new khedive was openly critical of the British occupiers, especially of Lord Cromer, who essentially had a free hand in Egyptian politics. Moreover, the British managed to install a pro-British prime minister of Egypt, Mustafa Fahmi Pasha, who would serve until 1908, with a two-year break between 1893 and 1895. Mustafa Fahmi Pasha eventually became Britain's direct puppet in the khedivate, which allowed the British to have more leverage in the country's internal affairs.

The main objective of the British in Egypt during this period was undermining the young and underdeveloped nationalist movement, which was headed by a lawyer and journalist named Mustafa Kamil, who studied in France and returned to Egypt in 1894. As one of the most vocal critics of the occupation, he founded the newspaper *Al-Liwa* in the year 1900, which became one of the main channels of Egyptian nationalists at the time. In his many speeches and writings, the young activist called for the Egyptian people to find their old strength and resilience and overthrow the yoke of the foreigners in the spirit of their ancestors who had done so many times. Mustafa Kamil also viewed the khedive as the leader of the future Egyptian state after the end of the British occupation and favored closer contact with the Ottomans—a fellow Muslim nation—if the choice between them and the British ever arose.

Egyptian nationalism saw a quick upsurge in the late 1890s before the British implemented countermeasures to prevent it from springing up again. In 1896, under the British high command, Egyptian forces launched a military campaign into Sudan, which had almost slipped away from Egyptian control in the previous years by the local Mahdi Muslims. The combined Anglo-Egyptian offensive was a success, taking Khartoum and largely putting an end to the Sudanese resistance by the end of the century. The victory briefly motivated the nationalists, who remembered the old days of their military's former glory. However, the British were quick to suppress any nationalist uprising that might have occurred due to the reconquest of Sudan. The Egyptians were excluded from the administration of the new territories, and Britain planned to eventually unite Egypt with its Sudanese territories into one large administrative unit.

By the dawn of the 20th century, everyone realized that tension was building between the Egyptian nationalists and the British, as the latter had shown increasing detachment from Egyptian affairs. This left many to wonder what the plans of the British were regarding their country. Khedive Abbas was still formally the ruler of the Ottoman province, though neither of them had any real say in politics. The British favored their own people in governmental and administrative posts instead of local Egyptians.

The tensions culminated in the so-called Denshawai incident, which took place in the summer of 1906. British soldiers at the Egyptian village of Denshawai got into a conflict with the local population, resulting in injuries to four locals, including one death. One British soldier also died, possibly of heatstroke since the villagers did not attack the soldiers. Surviving soldiers reported the incident to their officers, leading to the arrest of more than fifty of the village's inhabitants, all of whom were found guilty. The trial did not even last an hour. Some of the accused were put to death by hanging, while others got severe punishments, such as multiple-year terms in prison and whipping. The news of the incident soon spread among the Egyptian public. People were horrified by what had transpired at Denshawai and the fate of the villagers, nearly all of whom had been wrongfully accused. The domestic situation got increasingly tense, leading to Lord Cromer's resignation.

It became hard for Britain to accommodate the interests of the khedive's government amidst widespread public criticism. Anti-British sentiments were on the rise after the Denshawai incident, leading the British administration to consider granting the locals more say in their own affairs. Under Lord Kitchener, the British tried to implement policies that would affect the lower echelons of Egyptian society more and were careful to act in obvious opposition to the nationalists to dissuade more neutral or moderate Egyptians from joining the movement.

However, when World War One broke out in 1914, Great Britain and the Ottoman Empire became enemies. In November, the British declared war on the Ottomans and followed it up with the proclamation of a formal protectorate over Egypt. Control of the Suez during the war would prove crucial to the war effort of the Triple Entente (Russia, France, and the United Kingdom), although Egypt itself saw limited action during the war. The British also deposed Khedive Abbas II and installed his uncle, Hussein Kamel. The latter, on the orders of the British, declared independence from the Ottoman Empire and proclaimed himself the sultan of Egypt. Although the new Egyptian sultanate was a British protectorate, with the state apparatus and the military administered by the British, the Great War ended Ottoman control—however nominal it might have been for over a century—over Egypt. With the declaration of the protectorate in 1914, the modern era began in Egypt.

Chapter Eight – Modern Egypt

Throughout the 20th century, Egypt developed into both a nation with an identity of its own and a sovereign state. The fight for the advent of Egyptian nationhood and statehood was long and bloody, and violent and corrupt regimes were common throughout the 1900s.

The Kingdom of Egypt

The first sultan of the self-declared independent Sultanate of Egypt, Hussein Kamel, passed away in 1917 and was succeeded by his brother, Ahmad Fuad.

Throughout World War I, the international community had largely ignored the legal questions regarding Egypt's status as an ambiguous polity. However, these questions became more important as the war drew to a close and the winning powers had to decide what to do with the world. At the time, British Governor General Sir Reginal Wingate tried to limit the activities of Egyptian nationalists throughout the war. In 1918, he imprisoned the leader of the nationalist movement, Saad Zaghloul, who demanded Egypt's autonomy from both the Ottoman Empire and the protectorate. Zaghloul and other nationalists organized a delegation (a wafd) to London to bargain for the fate of their country. After initial resistance from

Saad Zaghloul, one of the original leaders of the Egyptian nationalist movement.[22]

the British against the demands of the nationalists, the Wafd transformed into a nationalist movement and organized Egyptian activists before emerging as a political party.

The end of World War I marked the beginning of a series of international conferences where diplomats from all over the world got to talk about the emerging world order after the collapse of the old one. With Egypt effectively being denied a seat at the negotiating table, protesters took to the streets against what they believed was an unjust British rule. Demonstrations in Egypt's biggest cities resulted in clashes with the local police and British troops, which tried to quell the revolts throughout 1919. The arrest of the Wafd Party leaders further motivated the protesters against the regime, with the situation escalating by November 1919. The British were forced to send another commission from London to deal with the matter. The commission was headed by Lord Alfred Milner. Milner and his group of bureaucrats arrived in Egypt after the people had boycotted the British administrators' plans to set up a quasi-government.

The Milner Commission evaluated the situation and communicated its severity to Lord Curzon, the British foreign secretary, who suggested changing the status of Egypt and relaxing British control. Zaghloul and the other members of the Wafd movement were released to lead the negotiations, and protests continued in the streets of Cairo, claiming the lives of hundreds of people. It was becoming more apparent that Egypt would not stop before it got its independence.

After extensive talks with the Wafd, the British administration in Egypt finally declared Egypt's independence on February 28th, 1922. Egypt was now a kingdom, a constitutional monarchy led by King Fuad, who would obtain his powers from the Constitution that was adopted in April of the following year. There was an important caveat, though. Britain retained the right to exercise influence over the different sectors of Egypt's political and socioeconomic life. For instance, Britain insisted that separate courts keep operating for foreigners in the country. It also remained in control of the Suez Canal and Sudan, as well as the country's communication infrastructure and military. British troops continued to be stationed on the borders of the independent Kingdom of Egypt.

King Fuad I of Egypt.[23]

Although Egypt would be proclaimed a constitutional monarchy, a democratic process according to the Constitution never happened. Three central political groups dominated the landscape: the nationalist Wafd movement, which supported full independence; King Fuad, who was afraid that he would lose his and his family's influence over Egypt; and Britain, which wished to continue its dominance and effective occupation of Egypt.

The Wafd, as the youngest of these forces, suffered the most in the first few years of Egyptian independence despite the fact that they kept winning the general elections. Saad Zaghloul and his numerous supporters, who had the harshest stance on the British occupation, continued to be silenced by the British as they tried to promote in-party rivalries and personal vendettas. This caused the Wafd to lose a large portion of its prominent members when it split off as an individual party, the Liberal Constitutionalists. Liberal Constitutionalist prime ministers were supported by the British but were disliked by the king, who dissolved the Egyptian Parliament in 1928, adding to the tension that existed among the country's largest political forces.

The intention of the British throughout the 1920s was to negotiate an official agreement with the Egyptian government that would guarantee optimal answers and solutions in favor of their interests. Negotiations were constantly being hindered because of the chaotic political process, with King Fuad coming out on top. In fact, when the Wafd Party boycotted the national elections in 1931, a decade after the proclamation of Egyptian independence, the situation was still not resolved. The main issue of contention was Sudan. The British wanted to get a deal that would give them full control over Sudan, something that was off the table for both the nationalists and the king. Meanwhile, the country continued to struggle economically, and general public opinion was directed against the British, whose forces continued to be stationed in key Egyptian cities.

It was only in the year 1936, with the passing of King Fuad and the accession of his young son Farouk I, that an agreement was reached with the British. The passing of the king had coincided with the general elections, which had been won, once again, by the Wafd nationalists. The political deadlock was broken with the signature of the Anglo-Egyptian Treaty in August, which was adopted and ratified in the wake of Britain's concerns with rising fascist Germany and Italy. In essence, it was a treaty of alliance, asserting the formal end of British occupation after more than half a century and Britain's right to maintain its soldiers in the Suez area to protect the canal. It also gave joint control of Britain and Egypt over Sudan. Despite the fact that the treaty was seen as a step forward to full Egyptian independence, the British presence would continue in Egypt with the aim of maintaining control over Britain's vast colonial empire.

This was the ongoing political climate in Egypt by the outbreak of World War II in 1939. Egypt was officially neutral during the conflict, but it aided Britain throughout the course of the war despite the fact there was a significant anti-British sentiment among the public. Even the Wafd, led by Mostafa el-Nahas, the prime minister who had negotiated the Anglo-Egyptian Treaty in 1936, cooperated with the British. Throughout his career, he served five times as the prime minister of Egypt, taking the office for the fourth time in 1942; he was dismissed by King Farouk two years later. The Egyptian forces did not fight, even as the Axis powers tried to invade Egypt, which was defended by British troops.

As the war came to a close and the Allied victory was imminent, the question of Egypt was at the top of the country's agenda. How would Egypt continue existing after all the British forces withdrew? What would the end of the war mean for Egyptian independence and the right to the self-determination of Egyptian people?

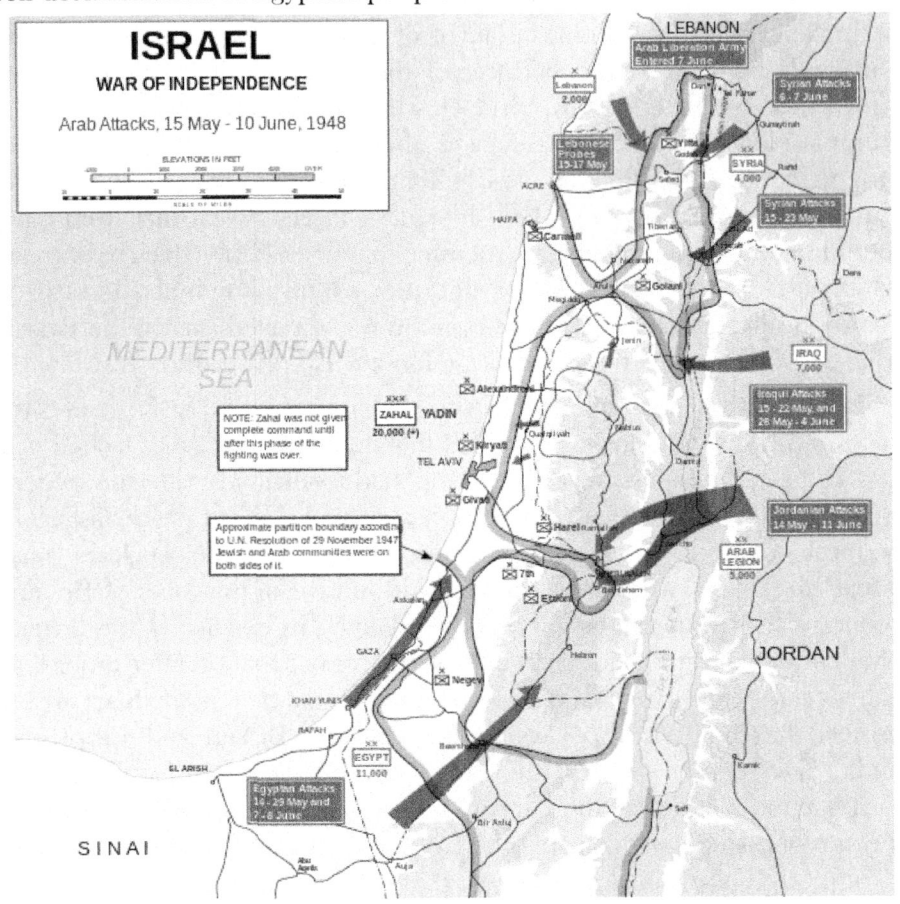

Offensives during the First Arab-Israeli War. (Note that the map says Israeli War of Independence, which is another name used to refer to the conflict.)[24]

The answers to these questions would be answered in the years following the end of the war, as the winning powers again tried to establish a stable international order with no place for the former European empires. Despite continued protests by the Egyptian people and efforts by the government, the British were reluctant to give up control of the Suez Canal, claiming that the British presence in the area was in the region's interests.

However, with the decision to establish the Jewish state of Israel in Palestine, anti-British sentiments continued to be voiced by the Egyptians and other Arab Muslim countries in the region. This led to the formation of the Arab League in March 1945, of which Egypt was a founding member. The aim of the Arab League was to coordinate the political actions of the Arab states and maintain stability. The country ultimately became involved in the first Arab-Israeli War in 1948, which broke out soon after the newly created United Nations adopted the resolution that divided Palestine into an Arab state and a Jewish state. Israel was targeted not only by Egypt but also by Jordan, Syria, Lebanon, and Iraq, who dispatched their forces in May 1948.

After about ten months of fighting, Israel emerged victorious, managing to take over more territories than had been assigned to it by the UN and beginning their military occupation. The Israelis signed separate armistice agreements with their enemies. Although the war did not spell the end of hostilities in Palestine and the surrounding countries, the Egyptian public felt humiliated after the defeat. The nationalists, led by Mostafa el-Nahas of the Wafd Party, won decisively in the 1950 elections and proceeded to withdraw from the 1936 Anglo-Egyptian Treaty in 1951. The nationalist government demanded that Britain withdraw its remaining forces from the Suez Canal and hand over control. Public pressure was growing, and the international eye was fixed on the events. Egyptian and British forces were mobilized at the Suez in October. This continued for months, as neither side backed down, leading to the breakout of fighting in early 1952.

Revolution

In January 1952, the British troops at the Suez, numbering up to seven thousand men, ordered the local Egyptian police officers, who were part of the standoff between the two countries, to surrender their weapons, which they refused. The British, themselves harassed many times during the months of conflict by Egyptian guerilla fighters and saboteurs, opened fire, which led to more than fifty Egyptian deaths.

The news of the fighting spread quickly, resulting in another wave of mass protests in Cairo that caused riots and clashes between activists and the police. The protests were mainly anti-British in nature, mixed with nationalist, Islamist, and pan-Arab elements. January 26th would become known as Black Saturday, with protests resulting in a fire that burned down much of old Cairo. More than five hundred people were injured. The city and the whole nation were in chaos.

Amidst the protests, King Farouk dissolved the government and dismissed Prime Minister el-Nahas from what had been his fifth and final term. By mid-July of 1952, three different emergency governments had been set up to deal with the growing instability, all of which had largely failed, causing more chaos in the streets. The situation was volatile, and there was talk of a conspiracy that wished to depose the king. The revolution would come in the summer of 1952 when a group of high-ranking Egyptian military commanders known as the Free Officers instigated a successful coup on July 23rd against the monarchy.

The Free Officers movement had been a largely underground organization. It was formed in the late 1940s after the humiliating defeat of Egypt in the first Arab-Israeli War. Its members had been military officials who believed that the existing political situation had brought nothing but problems for Egypt. They wanted to drive out both the king and the British from the country.

The instigators of the coup envisioned a complete restructuring of Egypt's political and social landscape, largely to root out existing problems like corruption. The Revolution of 1952 marked the transition of Egypt from a constitutional monarchy to a republic, though what form the republicanism brought by the Free Officers would adopt was still a question that was up in the air.

By that point, several prominent political forces had existed in Egypt. The first was the Wafd Party, the nationalist party that had ruled Egypt for most of the last decade. The communist Democratic Movement for National Liberation (DMNL) had also gained a bit of support in the country following the events of 1948. There was also the Muslim Brotherhood, a pan-Islamic fundamentalist movement that emerged in the 1920s and was largely opposed to foreign influence in Egypt and the formation of a secular state by Egyptian nationalists. As the provisional government set up by the Free Officers after the revolution in July prepared to work on the country's new constitution, these political groups were increasingly stigmatized and discriminated against.

The Free Officers set up the Revolutionary Command Council (RCC) to oversee the reinstatement of political order in the country following the revolution. The RCC put the country's former prime minister, Ali Maher, back in charge of leading a civilian cabinet of ministers and working on implementing the most pressing reforms. In January 1952, the RCC banned all political parties and created the Liberation Front, a broad and ambiguous movement that envisioned the unification of all political groups in one. It was becoming clear that Egypt was not moving toward establishing a democratic regime following the revolution.

Soon enough, there were conflicts among the leadership of the Free Officers. Colonel Gamal Abdel Nasser, one of the masterminds behind the movement, managed to outmaneuver his co-conspirators and gained too much power within the RCC. Nasser's main target was Major General Muhammad Naguib, a prominent face among the Free Officers who had served as president since the proclamation of the republic. In-party conflicts led to Naguib's resignation, and he was put under house arrest by Nasser and his allies. Nasser became the new chairman of the RCC.

The RCC continued to negotiate with the British about the occupation, and the talks resulted in an agreement in 1953 to inaugurate a three-year period after which Sudan would become independent. Under the 1954 Anglo-Egyptian Treaty, all British forces were to leave the Suez Canal by June 1956. Another victory was claimed by Nasser after an assassination attempt by a member of the radical Muslim Brotherhood failed in October 1954. Nasser retaliated by arresting thousands of members of the organization, including those suspected of cooperating with it.

Leaders of the 1952 Revolution, Gamal Abdel Nasser and Muhammad Naguib, photographed in a Cadillac after the revolution.[25]

Nasser's ascendancy to power was completed in 1956. The reorganized Liberal Front (now called the National Union, or NU) organized a referendum on whether to promulgate a newly drafted constitution and make Nasser president. On June 23rd, both proposals were approved by Egyptian voters. There were mixed feelings about the Constitution of 1956. It made Egypt into a presidential republic with a 350-member legislative body called the National Assembly, whose members were to be approved by the president before they could begin their activities. The Constitution also established a secular regime in Egypt, allowing for extensive women's rights, including the right to vote.

What made Nasser's presidency especially intriguing for the international community was his unreliable stance on foreign and security policy. This stemmed from Nasser's inability to resolve the issue of pan-Arabism and Egyptian nationalism (about whether or not the two concepts were mutually beneficial or opposed to each other). For instance, in February of 1955, a large-scale Israeli airstrike in the Egyptian-controlled Gaza Strip killed thirty-eight Egyptians. Nasser did not retaliate by declaring war. Israel's actions had been in response to the raids organized on its citizens by Palestinian fedayeen (guerilla fighter) groups. Inaction from Nasser was interpreted as a sign of weakness. Nasser's actions were closely surveyed because of the ideological conflict between the capitalist West and the communist Soviet Union.

Nasser did not join the new anti-communist Baghdad Pact, a treaty organization formed by Turkey, Pakistan, Iraq, and Iran, which was supported by the UK and the US. Nasser had unsuccessfully tried to purchase weapons from the Western powers, leading him to strike a lucrative arms deal with communist Czechoslovakia. Egypt was now to be supplied with Soviet-made military equipment. Western propaganda began to depict Nasser as a threat to democracy and capitalism in the Arab world despite the fact that the Egyptian president was one of the founding members of the Non-Aligned Movement, alongside Yugoslavia and India in 1956. The Non-Aligned Movement was formally established to emphasize that participating countries did not wish to align themselves with either the West or the Soviets in the Cold War.

Tensions between Nasser's regime and the West escalated in the Suez Crisis in 1956. Because of the Egyptian president's increasing anti-Western rhetoric, support for the Algerian nationalists in their struggle against France, and nominal "non-alignment" in the struggle against the communists, Western powers thought of Nasser as a potential threat.

Clashes between the Israelis and the Palestinians from the Egyptian-controlled Gaza Strip were becoming more and more frequent. In fact, Egypt enforced a naval blockade of Israel by blocking the Straits of Tiran in the Red Sea. In June 1956, the United States decided to pull its proposed financial support for the construction of the Aswan Dam, a project that would have greatly boosted Egypt's energy resources and created thousands of jobs in the Egyptian market. Furious by the decision, Nasser, who was supported overwhelmingly by the public at home, proceeded to nationalize the Suez Canal Company, the same French company that had run the canal since its construction. The nationalization of the company meant huge financial losses for the British and the French, both of which had huge stakes in it.

On October 29th, 1956, Israel invaded Egypt with the aim of ending the blockade. On November 5th, after the calls for a ceasefire were rejected, both France and Britain joined Israel's side and sent forces to join the fighting on the Sinai Peninsula. Egypt was about to fight a full-scale war against three nations, but international pressure, primarily from the United States, forced the Europeans to back down and led to the negotiation of a ceasefire between all belligerents. The United Nations issued a resolution that forced Britain, France, and Israel to remove their troops from the Suez Canal, which continued to be under Nasser's control. The incident became known as the Suez Crisis, and it was perceived as an Egyptian victory despite hundreds of casualties in just over a week of fighting.

By the second half of the 1950s, Nasser had given rise to what has since been dubbed Arab socialism, the ideology that postulated Arab nationalists throughout the Arab world had been fighting for the establishment of liberal and socialist regimes in their country. This statement was mostly true, as the main intent of nationalists in the Arab countries was to fight against European imperialism, promote the interests of the lower social classes, and get rid of the existing largely conservative regimes. Pan-Arabism, the ideology that emphasized the need for all Arab states to work together in the post-war world, largely aligned with this concept, and both were increasingly upheld by Nasser in his speeches and his actions. Nasser was already seen as a staunch resistor of foreign influences because of his involvement in the international Non-Aligned Movement, as well as the Suez Crisis.

In 1958, trying to further build up this image, Nasser agreed to incorporate the territories of Syria at the request of the Pan-Arabist Syrian government, which had requested a union of the two countries. The request came after years of political instability in Syria, with the country being unable to maintain order since its independence. The United Arab Republic (UAR) was created on February 1st, 1958, with Nasser at its helm. This was a hasty move by the Egyptian president, who could not manage to effectively integrate the two countries under one administration. The Syrians were unjustly discriminated against under the United Arab Republic, leading to a military coup in the country and the subsequent secession of Syria from the UAR in the summer of 1961. Despite this, Egypt retained the name for another ten years.

Domestically, Nasser's pan-Arabic and Arab socialist leanings were manifested in another reorganization of the National Union party into the Arab Socialist Union (ASU). Nasser was careful not to call himself a communist leader, though he implemented increasingly leftist policies and forged closer ties with the Soviets. After the Revolution of 1952, Egypt steadily grew its economy, partly thanks to the leftist policies enacted by the president. Between 1962 and 1967, the UAR intervened on the side of the Yemeni republicans, who had been fighting against the monarchy, in the Yemeni Civil War.

The biggest shortcoming of Nasser's rule was his stance against Israel. He was accused of being too passive by the other Arab nations in the region. Palestinian Arabs, who had been forcefully deported or had to migrate from Palestine after the creation of the Jewish state, had not ceased their hostile activities against the Israelis. They operated from the territories under occupation and also from neighboring Arab countries, leading to several instances of military retaliation by Israel. The situation was relatively stable between Israel and Egypt, as the UNEF (United Nations Emergency Force) worked to maintain peace in the Sinai Peninsula.

In late 1966, Israel launched deadly strikes on Jordan. In May 1967, Egypt mobilized 100,000 soldiers on the Israeli border after forcing the UNEF forces to withdraw. This was followed by the reestablishment of the blockade of the Straits of Tiran against Israel, something that effectively meant a declaration of war according to international law. Nasser was finally giving in to the pressure from other Arab countries.

In early June, Jordan and Egypt signed a defensive alliance. The Israeli high command made a critical decision to launch a surprise airstrike against Egypt. The Israeli Air Force (IAF) managed to quickly take out key targets of the Egyptian Air Force, destroying most of the planes and vital airfields. This was a huge hit to Egypt's military capabilities, as the Israelis also launched attacks on Egyptian forces in the Sinai and achieved victories because of a lack of aerial support for Egypt. The IAF then proceeded to strike Syria, Jordan, and Iraq, achieving quick success in the short conflict that became known as the Six-Day War. A ceasefire agreement was reached by the belligerents and was signed on June 11th. With this defeat, it became clear that the days of Gamal Abdel Nasser in office were coming to an end.

From Sadat to Mubarak to the Arab Spring

In the aftermath of the Six-Day War, Israel occupied the Gaza Strip and the Sinai Peninsula. The defeat in the war had broken President Nasser, who assumed both the position of prime minister and supreme commander of Egypt's armed forces following the defeat. This move was done to strengthen his image and adopt rapid and effective changes. In the summer of 1967, representatives of the Arab League met in Khartoum to discuss their common policy against Israel. Their decision was a unilateral denouncement of Israel's actions and the so-called "three no's" resolution—no recognition, no peace, and no relations with the state of Israel.

Sporadic fighting between the Arab nations and Israel continued in the Sinai until 1970 and ended with the death of the Egyptian president. On September 28th, 1970, Gamal Abdel Nasser suffered a heart attack after the end of the Arab League's meeting, where he had managed to broker a peace agreement between the government of Jordan and the Palestinian Liberation Organization. The loss of the president was mourned not only by Egypt but also by the rest of the Arab world. President Nasser was a compelling figure and, in the eyes of many, the savior of modern Egypt. His funeral procession in Cairo was attended by an estimated five million people.

Vice President Anwar Sadat replaced Nasser as the country's interim president. Sadat was an experienced politician and public figure, having served in the country's wars and having been part of the original Free Officers movement that overthrew the monarchy in 1952. Filling in Nasser's shoes was no easy task, but as time would tell, Sadat was able to quickly consolidate his power and outmaneuver his political rivals, emerging on top in just two years. Proclaiming the inauguration of what he called the Corrective Revolution in May 1971, Sadat proceeded to purge his political opponents. His actions were primarily directed at limiting socialist and Arab socialist (those who advocated for pan-Arabism) members within the government and the armed forces. This marked the beginning of drastic changes in Egypt's domestic and foreign policy under Sadat's presidency, which would last until 1981. Sadat was more of a center-right, pragmatic politician, and his measures eventually reduced the influence of Nasserism, the word often used to refer to the political ideology and direction Egypt had taken under President Nasser.

Perhaps nothing describes the change of style under the new president better than the War of Yom Kippur, another Egyptian-Israeli conflict. It began on October 6th, 1973. Sadat, having secretly planned to invade Israel with Syrian President Hafez al-Assad, primarily wished to reinstate control over the Sinai Peninsula. The Syrians were after the Golan Heights region in northeastern Israel.

The Israelis were celebrating one of the most important Jewish holidays, Yom Kippur, so they were caught completely off-guard. The Arab forces achieved early victories. The Israeli forces began to retaliate, bombarding Syria with artillery, crossing the Suez Canal, and counter-invading Egypt. A ceasefire agreement was finally reached on October 25th after mediation and involvement of the United States, which had provided military aid to Israel by air. The UN ceasefire resolution that had been issued earlier had been ignored by both sides.

The ceasefire agreement had been reached at a moment when both forces had advanced into enemy

President Anwar Sadat.[26]

territory, leading to the creation of temporary occupation zones before the peace talks continued. Negotiations dragged on for years as both sides analyzed the outcome of the conflict. President Sadat believed it to have been a great Egyptian victory and emphasized the fact that Egypt was in a leading position in the peace talks. In the following years, the countries agreed to withdraw forces from the Sinai, but it was not until September of 1978 that formal peace between the two sides was achieved. The Camp

David Accords, as the treaty became known, were negotiated between President Sadat and Israeli Prime Minister Menachem Begin and were mediated by US President Jimmy Carter.

The Camp David Accords were a massive step in normalizing relations between Israel and Egypt. They outlined the terms of the peace with regard to the demilitarization of parts of the Sinai Peninsula and also built a framework for future relations between the countries and security in the region. It was the most profound development for fostering peace between Israel and the Arab world, earning both heads of state the Nobel Prize for Peace. In fact, the move was so unexpected that the Arab nations denounced Egypt's actions and expelled the country from the Arab League to show their dissatisfaction with Sadat.

Domestically, Sadat pursued an "open door" economic policy called the Infitah, which was aimed at attracting private investment by breaking down some of the bureaucratic barriers created under Nasser's presidency. Many socialist and Nasserist policies began to be reversed, and liberalization of the political landscape of the country was encouraged, with political parties being made legal again. However, most Egyptians continued to struggle economically and were largely unaffected by the changes in the fiscal bureaucracy. Hardships led many to protest against Sadat's government.

Sadat's anti-socialist measures resulted in the growth of radical movements such as the Muslim Brotherhood. Many activists were released from prison and rejoined the public discourse, where they found widespread but largely tacit support. More importantly, the 1970s saw an increase in Islamist terrorist activities in Egypt, which were largely driven by the accommodations given to the Muslim Brotherhood and the smaller underground organizations that had formed under Sadat.

On October 6th, 1981, President Sadat was assassinated by Khalid al-Islambouli, a lieutenant in the Egyptian army who had joined the radical Egyptian Islamic Jihad group. The group had formed in the late 1970s and managed to forge contacts with members of the Egyptian military, which supplied it with weapons through corrupt channels. The leaders of the organization had declared their intent to kill the leaders of the country and establish a conservative Islamic regime, leading to the arrest of hundreds of its members, supporters, and suspected associates by the Egyptian police in February 1981. Twelve people, including President Sadat and foreign diplomats, were killed on October 6th as the president and his guests were celebrating the anniversary of the beginning of the Yom Kippur War of 1973. Twenty-eight people were wounded. Among them was the next president of Egypt, Hosni Mubarak.

Mubarak had been the vice president since 1975 and held a popular position among Egypt's elite and the people, as he had also served as the commander of Egypt's air force during the war in 1973. Mubarak's long tenure as president came to an end in 2011. His tenure would mark a transformative episode for modern Egypt. The Egyptian nationalist movement matured, and different social forces developed their visions for the country's future. In fact, Mubarak managed to reassert Egypt's reputation as the center of the Arab world, which had been in tatters since peace had been negotiated—at least in the eyes of the Arab countries. Mubarak was able to restore cordial relations with the other members of the Arab League, leading to Egypt's reinstatement as a member and the return of the organization's headquarters to Cairo.

Hosni Mubarak.[27]

Domestically, however, Mubarak's term as president did not bring much prosperity to the Egyptian people, who had to experience living in an increasingly authoritarian, undemocratic, and poor country. To tackle the problems of the Egyptian economy, Mubarak encouraged large private investments and further cut the public sector, something that created extra money in the budget. Throughout his presidency, Egypt had to increasingly rely on foreign loans, as the country's currency continued to be devalued to combat inflation and keep its rate in the single digits. The oil crisis of the 1980s hit Egypt hard, forcing many out of jobs and into poverty. The Egyptian economy showed some signs of life during the 1990s, as Egypt fought on the side of the US-led coalition in the Gulf War in 1991 in exchange for the pardon of much of its foreign debt. Billions of dollars were forgiven, and Egypt's GDP experienced a period of growth. However, that growth was not utilized effectively to affect the lives of ordinary Egyptians.

Meanwhile, Mubarak became an authoritarian leader who ruled by decree. For example, presidential referendums were held in 1987, 1993, and 1997, but he was the only candidate. He cracked down on political dissidents and restricted the freedom of the press, coming under increasing international scrutiny in the 1990s.

Rising wealth inequality and poor living conditions forced many Egyptians to seek refuge in the "protective arms" of Islamist terrorist organizations, which experienced massive growth under Mubarak. Disenchanted Egyptians were often attracted to these groups since they were staunch opponents of Mubarak and had a clear vision of the future of a strong Arab world. The growth of such groups persisted despite Mubarak's regime's continued efforts to suppress Islamist organizations, which included preventive arrests based on suspicion and the use of torture during interrogations. Throughout the 1990s, few people dared to publicly proclaim their Islamist sympathies, afraid of being targeted by the government.

Terrorists increased their activities, targeting both government officials and civilians. They nearly succeeded in assassinating President Mubarak during his visit to the Ethiopian capital of Addis Ababa in 1995. Egypt became a hotbed for Islamist terrorism. The international community was still learning how to combat non-state actors, such as radical groups that incited people to commit violence and justified their actions with religion. As the radical Islamist terrorist groups grew in size and became more prominent in the Arab world, the Muslim Brotherhood and its associates were confident enough to transform into full-fledged political parties.

By the 2000s, dissent among the Egyptian people was growing. It was only after heavy international scrutiny that President Mubarak allowed other candidates to participate in the 2005 presidential referendum, which he still won by a landslide. Parliamentary elections had been held five years earlier, and Mubarak's National Democratic Party secured a clear majority. Effectively, the state and government apparatus remained in the hands of the president and his allies, and corrupt officials perpetuated the authoritarian rule of Mubarak. Living under repressive conditions made many Egyptians disillusioned with the government, which continued to silence any voices critical of it. Egyptian opposition remained disorganized, though, with only the Muslim Brotherhood being a clear opponent. It secured about a fifth of the votes in the parliamentary elections.

Conclusion – The Arab Spring and the Future of Egypt

Hosni Mubarak was forced to resign in February 2011 after a series of large demonstrations and protests against his regime that had begun in late January. The activists were upset by Mubarak's authoritarian rule, the police brutality that had been endorsed by the government, the lack of freedom of expression and the press, and the growing economic difficulties. The wave of protests was sparked by the events in Tunisia, where disenchantment with the rule of Tunisian dictator Zine El Abidine Ben Ali led to the Jasmine Revolution. Hundreds of thousands of protesters assembled over the course of a couple of days in the streets of Cairo in late January. Their main demand was Mubarak's resignation and the holding of free and fair elections in the country. The Muslim Brotherhood, the biggest opposition political force, joined the demonstrations, as did other parties.

The protesters paralyzed the city, resulting in clashes with the police officers ordered to suppress the demonstrators. Tahrir Square in Cairo became their center of operations. Interestingly, the protesters had assembled on their own without any particular persona leading them. As clashes with the police intensified and riots broke out in prison, adding to the severity of the situation, decisive action had to be taken. The president asked the armed forces for help in dispersing the protestors, but many soldiers were overwhelmingly on the side of the people, sharing many of their grievances and refusing to use violence against the public.

On February 11th, Vice President Omar Suleiman broke the news of Hosni Mubarak's resignation. Power was transferred to the Supreme Council of the Armed Forces, which announced its plans for a transitional government and elections. The streets of Cairo rejoiced. Thousands of people had been injured and arrested during the Egyptian Revolution of 2011, and over eight hundred people had been killed. In addition to Egypt and Tunisia, similar mass protests erupted throughout the rest of the Arab world in 2011. This event has become known as the Arab Spring.

The Arab Spring led to the election of conservative Mohamed Morsi as the president in the 2012 presidential elections. However, the new government was unable to address many of the problems the Egyptian people had, leading to another wave of mass protests in June 2013. Morsi was deposed by a military coup led by General Abdel Fattah al-Sisi, who eventually became president after elections were held a year later. Although military rule has led to relative stability, Sisi's presidency is also marked by the return of harsh authoritarian policies reminiscent of Mubarak's rule. Political and socioeconomic grievances continue to haunt the Egyptian population, and the military is actively involved in the state apparatus.

The Arab Spring serves as a great conclusion to the history of Egypt. The long-term effects of the protests resulted in the toppling of dictatorships throughout the Arab world, and the effects are still continuing to be seen today. One thing is for sure: the aftermath of the Revolution of 2011 did not really change much for the people, which many would say has been the case for most of Egypt's 20th-century history. The political, social, and economic problems in Egypt today largely stem from the meddling of foreign influences in the country's domestic affairs.

The history of Egypt shows us the evolution of one of the first civilizations in the world into the largest Arab nation in the world. In a way, Egyptians have never lost the sense of grandeur and pride of the Egyptian civilization. At different points in time, Egyptians considered themselves the continuers of the tradition of great leaders such as Ramesses II, Alexander the Great, and Saladin, and modern-day Egyptians have a right to claim this tradition. As Egypt continues to navigate its way through a rapidly changing world, the Egyptian people, with their unique culture, way of life, and sense of unity, will play a decisive role in ending the centuries-long struggle of searching for their identity.

If you enjoyed this book, a review on Amazon would be greatly appreciated because it would mean a lot to hear from you.

To leave a review:
1. Open your camera app.
2. Point your mobile device at the QR code.
3. The review page will appear in your web browser.

Thanks for your support!

Here's another book by Captivating History that you might like

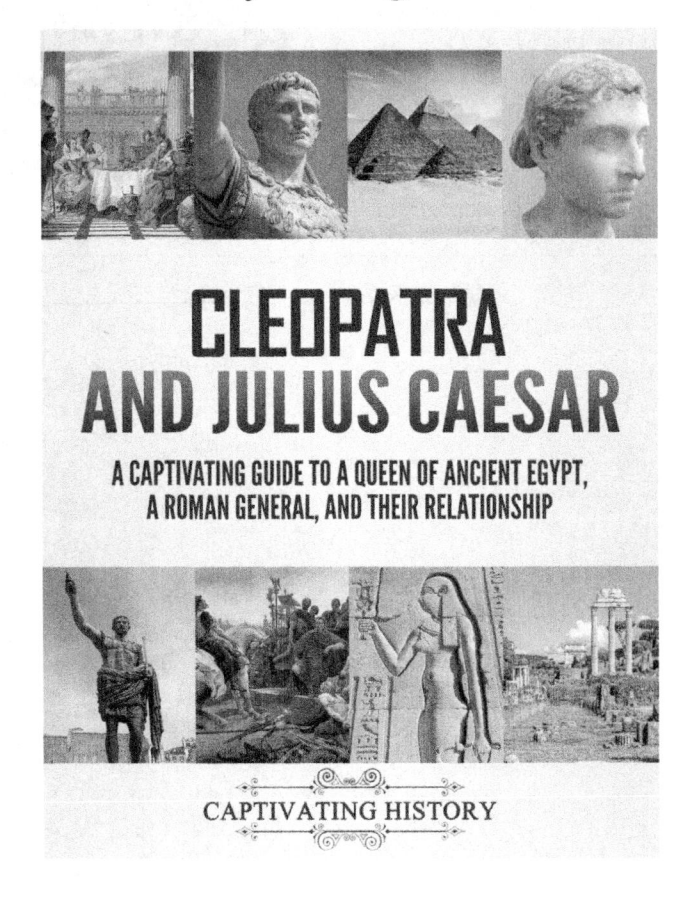

CLEOPATRA AND JULIUS CAESAR

A CAPTIVATING GUIDE TO A QUEEN OF ANCIENT EGYPT, A ROMAN GENERAL, AND THEIR RELATIONSHIP

CAPTIVATING HISTORY

Free Bonus from Captivating History (Available for a Limited time)

Hi History Lovers!

Now you have a chance to join our exclusive history list so you can get your first history ebook for free as well as discounts and a potential to get more history books for free!

Simply visit the link below to join.

Or, Scan the QR code!

captivatinghistory.com/ebook

Also, make sure to follow us on Facebook, X, and YouTube by searching for Captivating History.

Sources

Bellin, E. (2012). Reconsidering the Robustness of Authoritarianism in the Middle East: Lessons from the Arab Spring. *Comparative Politics, 44*(2), 127-149. http://www.jstor.org/stable/23211807

Bickerton, I.J., & Klausner, C.L. (2017). A History of the Arab-Israeli Conflict (8th ed.). Routledge. https://doi.org/10.4324/9781315100241

Bowman, A. K., & Rathbone, D. (1992). Cities and Administration in Roman Egypt. *The Journal of Roman Studies, 82*, 107-127. https://doi.org/10.2307/301287

Breasted, J. H. (2015). *A history of Egypt : from the earliest times to the Persian conquest / James Henry Breasted.* Cambridge University Press.

BROWNLEE, J. (2011). Peace Before Freedom: Diplomacy and Repression in Sadat's Egypt. *Political Science Quarterly, 126*(4), 641-668. http://www.jstor.org/stable/41502471

Ğabra, Ğaudat. (2014). *Coptic civilization : two thousand years of Christianity in Egypt / ed. by Gawdat Gabra.* The American Univ. in Cairo Press.

Ghanem, H. (2016). Roots of the Arab Spring. In *The Arab Spring Five Years Later: Toward Greater Inclusiveness* (pp. 39-64). Brookings Institution Press. http://www.jstor.org/stable/10.7864/j.ctt1657tv8.6

Hanna, N. (2014). *Ottoman Egypt and the emergence of the modern world, 1500-1800 / Nelly Hanna.* (1st ed.). The American University in Cairo Press.

Kemp, B., & Zink, A. (2012). Life in Ancient Egypt Akhentanen, the Amarna Period, and Tutankhamun. *RCC Perspectives, 3*, 9-24. http://www.jstor.org/stable/26240370

Lesko, B. S. (1991). Women's Monumental Mark on Ancient Egypt. *The Biblical Archaeologist, 54*(1), 4-15. https://doi.org/10.2307/3210327

Mahaffy, J. P. (John P. (2014). *A history of Egypt. Volume 4, Under the Ptolemaic dynasty / John Pentland Mahaff.* Cambridge University Press.

Marwa El Ashmouni, & Katharine Bartsch. (2014). Egypt's Age of Transition: Unintentional Cosmopolitanism during the Reign of Muhammad 'Alī (1805-1848). *Arab Studies Quarterly, 36*(1), 43-74. https://doi.org/10.13169/arabstudquar.36.1.0043

Petry, C. F. (Ed.). (1998). *The Cambridge history of Egypt. Volume 1, 640-1517 / edited by Carl F. Petry.* Cambridge University Press.

Rubin, B. (1991). Pan-Arab Nationalism: The Ideological Dream as Compelling Force. *Journal of Contemporary History, 26*(3/4), 535-551. http://www.jstor.org/stable/260659

Safty, A. (1991). Sadat's Negotiations with the United States and Israel: From Sinai to Camp David. *The American Journal of Economics and Sociology, 50*(3), 285-298. http://www.jstor.org/stable/3487270

Sayyid-Marsot, A. L., & Sayyid-Marsot, A. Lutfi. (2007). *A History of Egypt: From the Arab Conquest to the Present / Afaf Lutfi Al-Sayyid Marsot* (Second edition.). Cambridge University Press.

Shaw, I. (Ed.). (2003). *The Oxford History of Ancient Egypt [Electronic Resource] / edited by Ian Shaw.* Oxford University Press.

Shehata, D. (2011). The Fall of the Pharaoh: How Hosni Mubarak's Reign Came to an End. *Foreign Affairs, 90*(3), 26-32. http://www.jstor.org/stable/23039404

Van de Mieroop, M. (2011). *A History of Ancient Egypt / Marc Van De Mieroop.* (1. publ.). Wiley-Blackwell.

Image Sources

[1] https://commons.wikimedia.org/wiki/File:Narmer_Palette.jpg

[2] https://commons.wikimedia.org/wiki/File:De_trappiramide_van_Djoser_te_Sakkara,_Egypte,_1916,_SFA001009957.jpg

[3] Robster1983 at English Wikipedia, CC0, via Wikimedia Commons; https://commons.wikimedia.org/wiki/File:Giza-pyramids.JPG

[4] https://commons.wikimedia.org/wiki/File:Thutmosis_III-2.jpg

[5] Brooklyn Museum, No restrictions, via Wikimedia Commons; https://commons.wikimedia.org/wiki/File:Antonio_Beato,_Colosses_de_Memnon,_19th_century.jpg

[6] https://commons.wikimedia.org/wiki/File:Spaziergang_im_Garten_Amarna_Berlin.jpg

[7] https://commons.wikimedia.org/wiki/File:Amarna_Akkadian_letter.png

[8] https://commons.wikimedia.org/wiki/File:Tuts_Tomb_Opened.JPG

[9] ArdadN, Jeff Dahl, CC BY-SA 3.0 <https://creativecommons.org/licenses/by-sa/3.0>, via Wikimedia Commons; https://commons.wikimedia.org/wiki/File:Egypt_NK_edit.svg

[10] Olaf Tausch, CC BY 3.0 <https://creativecommons.org/licenses/by/3.0>, via Wikimedia Commons; https://commons.wikimedia.org/wiki/File:Gro%C3%9Fer_Tempel_(Abu_Simbel)_31.jpg

[11] Jeff Dahl, CC BY-SA 4.0 <https://creativecommons.org/licenses/by-sa/4.0>, via Wikimedia Commons; https://commons.wikimedia.org/wiki/File:Third_Intermediate_Period_map.svg

[12] Original creator: MossmapsCorrections according to Oxford Atlas of World History 2002, The Times Atlas of World History (1989), Philip's Atlas of World History (1999) by 7, CC BY-SA 4.0 <https://creativecommons.org/licenses/by-sa/4.0>, via Wikimedia Commons; https://commons.wikimedia.org/wiki/Category:Maps_of_the_Achaemenid_Empire#/media/File:Ac

haemenid Empire at its greatest extent according to Oxford Atlas of World History_2002.jpg

[13] https://commons.wikimedia.org/wiki/File:Ptolemy_I_Soter_Louvre_Ma849.jpg

[14] https://commons.wikimedia.org/wiki/File:Kleopatra-VII.-Altes-Museum-Berlin1.jpg

[15] Cristiano64, CC BY-SA 3.0 <http://creativecommons.org/licenses/by-sa/3.0/>, via Wikimedia Commons; https://commons.wikimedia.org/wiki/File:Impero_romano_sotto_Ottaviano_Augusto_30aC_-_6dC.jpg

[16] https://commons.wikimedia.org/wiki/File:Map_of_expansion_of_Caliphate.svg

[17] Ro4444, CC BY-SA 4.0 <https://creativecommons.org/licenses/by-sa/4.0>, via Wikimedia Commons; https://commons.wikimedia.org/wiki/File:Ayyubid_Sultanate_1193_AD.jpg

[18] https://commons.wikimedia.org/wiki/File:Mameluke-in-Full-Armour.jpg

[19] https://commons.wikimedia.org/wiki/File:ModernEgypt,_Muhammad_Ali_by_Auguste_Couder,_BAP_17996.jpg

[20] Don-kun, Eric Gaba (Sting - fr:Sting), CC BY 3.0 <https://creativecommons.org/licenses/by/3.0>, via Wikimedia Commons; https://commons.wikimedia.org/wiki/File:Egypt_under_Muhammad_Ali_Dynasty_map_en.png

[21] https://commons.wikimedia.org/wiki/File:Tewfik_Pasha.jpg

[22] https://commons.wikimedia.org/wiki/File:ModernEgypt,_Saad_Zaghloul,_BAP_14785.jpg

[23] https://commons.wikimedia.org/wiki/File:Fuad_I_of_Egypt.jpg

[24] https://commons.wikimedia.org/wiki/File:1948_Arab_Israeli_War_-_May_15-June_10.svg

[25] https://commons.wikimedia.org/wiki/File:Nasser_and_Naguib,_1954.jpg

[26] https://commons.wikimedia.org/wiki/File:Anwar_Sadat_cropped.jpg

[27] https://commons.wikimedia.org/wiki/File:Hosni_Mubarak_-_Official_Photo.JPG

Printed in Great Britain
by Amazon